FREE Study Skills Videos/DVD Offer

Dear Customer,

Thank you for your purchase from Mometrix! We consider it an honor and a privilege that you have purchased our product and we want to ensure your satisfaction.

As a way of showing our appreciation and to help us better serve you, we have developed Study Skills Videos that we would like to give you for <u>FREE</u>. These videos cover our *best practices* for getting ready for your exam, from how to use our study materials to how to best prepare for the day of the test.

All that we ask is that you email us with feedback that would describe your experience so far with our product. Good, bad, or indifferent, we want to know what you think!

To get your FREE Study Skills Videos, you can use the **QR code** below, or send us an **email** at studyvideos@mometrix.com with *FREE VIDEOS* in the subject line and the following information in the body of the email:

- The name of the product you purchased.
- Your product rating on a scale of 1-5, with 5 being the highest rating.
- Your feedback. It can be long, short, or anything in between. We just want to know your impressions and experience so far with our product. (Good feedback might include how our study material met your needs and ways we might be able to make it even better. You could highlight features that you found helpful or features that you think we should add.)

If you have any questions or concerns, please don't hesitate to contact me directly.

Thanks again!

Sincerely,

Jay Willis
Vice President
jay.willis@mometrix.com
1-800-673-8175

Life & Health Exam

SECRETS

Study Guide
Your Key to Exam Success

Written and edited by the Mometrix Test Prep

Mometrix offers volume discount pricing to institutions. For more information or a price quote, please contact our sales department at sales@mometrix.com or 888-248-1219.

Paperback
ISBN 13: 978-1-60971-988-3
ISBN 10: 1-60971-988-3

Ebook
ISBN 13: 978-1-62120-310-0
ISBN 10: 1-62120-310-7

Hardback
ISBN 13: 978-1-5167-1377-6
ISBN 10: 1-5167-1377-X

DEAR FUTURE EXAM SUCCESS STORY

First of all, **THANK YOU** for purchasing Mometrix study materials!

Second, congratulations! You are one of the few determined test-takers who are committed to doing whatever it takes to excel on your exam. **You have come to the right place.** We developed these study materials with one goal in mind: to deliver you the information you need in a format that's concise and easy to use.

In addition to optimizing your guide for the content of the test, we've outlined our recommended steps for breaking down the preparation process into small, attainable goals so you can make sure you stay on track.

We've also analyzed the entire test-taking process, identifying the most common pitfalls and showing how you can overcome them and be ready for any curveball the test throws you.

Standardized testing is one of the biggest obstacles on your road to success, which only increases the importance of doing well in the high-pressure, high-stakes environment of test day. Your results on this test could have a significant impact on your future, and this guide provides the information and practical advice to help you achieve your full potential on test day.

Your success is our success

We would love to hear from you! If you would like to share the story of your exam success or if you have any questions or comments in regard to our products, please contact us at **800-673-8175** or **support@mometrix.com**.

Thanks again for your business and we wish you continued success!

Sincerely,
The Mometrix Test Preparation Team

> **Need more help? Check out our flashcards at:**
> **MometrixFlashcards.com/LifeHealth**

TABLE OF CONTENTS

Introduction

Thank you for purchasing this resource! You have made the choice to prepare yourself for a test that could have a huge impact on your future, and this guide is designed to help you be fully ready for test day. Obviously, it's important to have a solid understanding of the test material, but you also need to be prepared for the unique environment and stressors of the test, so that you can perform to the best of your abilities.

For this purpose, the first section that appears in this guide is the **Secret Keys**. We've devoted countless hours to meticulously researching what works and what doesn't, and we've boiled down our findings to the five most impactful steps you can take to improve your performance on the test. We start at the beginning with study planning and move through the preparation process, all the way to the testing strategies that will help you get the most out of what you know when you're finally sitting in front of the test.

We recommend that you start preparing for your test as far in advance as possible. However, if you've bought this guide as a last-minute study resource and only have a few days before your test, we recommend that you skip over the first two Secret Keys since they address a long-term study plan.

If you struggle with **test anxiety**, we strongly encourage you to check out our recommendations for how you can overcome it. Test anxiety is a formidable foe, but it can be beaten, and we want to make sure you have the tools you need to defeat it.

Secret Key #1 – Plan Big, Study Small

There's a lot riding on your performance. If you want to ace this test, you're going to need to keep your skills sharp and the material fresh in your mind. You need a plan that lets you review everything you need to know while still fitting in your schedule. We'll break this strategy down into three categories.

Information Organization

Start with the information you already have: the official test outline. From this, you can make a complete list of all the concepts you need to cover before the test. Organize these concepts into groups that can be studied together, and create a list of any related vocabulary you need to learn so you can brush up on any difficult terms. You'll want to keep this vocabulary list handy once you actually start studying since you may need to add to it along the way.

Time Management

Once you have your set of study concepts, decide how to spread them out over the time you have left before the test. Break your study plan into small, clear goals so you have a manageable task for each day and know exactly what you're doing. Then just focus on one small step at a time. When you manage your time this way, you don't need to spend hours at a time studying. Studying a small block of content for a short period each day helps you retain information better and avoid stressing over how much you have left to do. You can relax knowing that you have a plan to cover everything in time. In order for this strategy to be effective though, you have to start studying early and stick to your schedule. Avoid the exhaustion and futility that comes from last-minute cramming!

Study Environment

The environment you study in has a big impact on your learning. Studying in a coffee shop, while probably more enjoyable, is not likely to be as fruitful as studying in a quiet room. It's important to keep distractions to a minimum. You're only planning to study for a short block of time, so make the most of it. Don't pause to check your phone or get up to find a snack. It's also important to **avoid multitasking**. Research has consistently shown that multitasking will make your studying dramatically less effective. Your study area should also be comfortable and well-lit so you don't have the distraction of straining your eyes or sitting on an uncomfortable chair.

 The time of day you study is also important. You want to be rested and alert. Don't wait until just before bedtime. Study when you'll be most likely to comprehend and remember. Even better, if you know what time of day your test will be, set that time aside for study. That way your brain will be used to working on that subject at that specific time and you'll have a better chance of recalling information.

Finally, it can be helpful to team up with others who are studying for the same test. Your actual studying should be done in as isolated an environment as possible, but the work of organizing the information and setting up the study plan can be divided up. In between study sessions, you can discuss with your teammates the concepts that you're all studying and quiz each other on the details. Just be sure that your teammates are as serious about the test as you are. If you find that your study time is being replaced with social time, you might need to find a new team.

2

Secret Key #2 – Make Your Studying Count

You're devoting a lot of time and effort to preparing for this test, so you want to be absolutely certain it will pay off. This means doing more than just reading the content and hoping you can remember it on test day. It's important to make every minute of study count. There are two main areas you can focus on to make your studying count.

Retention

It doesn't matter how much time you study if you can't remember the material. You need to make sure you are retaining the concepts. To check your retention of the information you're learning, try recalling it at later times with minimal prompting. Try carrying around flashcards and glance at one or two from time to time or ask a friend who's also studying for the test to quiz you.

To enhance your retention, look for ways to put the information into practice so that you can apply it rather than simply recalling it. If you're using the information in practical ways, it will be much easier to remember. Similarly, it helps to solidify a concept in your mind if you're not only reading it to yourself but also explaining it to someone else. Ask a friend to let you teach them about a concept you're a little shaky on (or speak aloud to an imaginary audience if necessary). As you try to summarize, define, give examples, and answer your friend's questions, you'll understand the concepts better and they will stay with you longer. Finally, step back for a big picture view and ask yourself how each piece of information fits with the whole subject. When you link the different concepts together and see them working together as a whole, it's easier to remember the individual components.

Finally, practice showing your work on any multi-step problems, even if you're just studying. Writing out each step you take to solve a problem will help solidify the process in your mind, and you'll be more likely to remember it during the test.

Modality

Modality simply refers to the means or method by which you study. Choosing a study modality that fits your own individual learning style is crucial. No two people learn best in exactly the same way, so it's important to know your strengths and use them to your advantage.

For example, if you learn best by visualization, focus on visualizing a concept in your mind and draw an image or a diagram. Try color-coding your notes, illustrating them, or creating symbols that will trigger your mind to recall a learned concept. If you learn best by hearing or discussing information, find a study partner who learns the same way or read aloud to yourself. Think about how to put the information in your own words. Imagine that you are giving a lecture on the topic and record yourself so you can listen to it later.

For any learning style, flashcards can be helpful. Organize the information so you can take advantage of spare moments to review. Underline key words or phrases. Use different colors for different categories. Mnemonic devices (such as creating a short list in which every item starts with the same letter) can also help with retention. Find what works best for you and use it to store the information in your mind most effectively and easily.

3

Secret Key #3 – Practice the Right Way

Your success on test day depends not only on how many hours you put into preparing, but also on whether you prepared the right way. It's good to check along the way to see if your studying is paying off. One of the most effective ways to do this is by taking practice tests to evaluate your progress. Practice tests are useful because they show exactly where you need to improve. Every time you take a practice test, pay special attention to these three groups of questions:

- The questions you got wrong
- The questions you had to guess on, even if you guessed right
- The questions you found difficult or slow to work through

This will show you exactly what your weak areas are, and where you need to devote more study time. Ask yourself why each of these questions gave you trouble. Was it because you didn't understand the material? Was it because you didn't remember the vocabulary? Do you need more repetitions on this type of question to build speed and confidence? Dig into those questions and figure out how you can strengthen your weak areas as you go back to review the material.

 Additionally, many practice tests have a section explaining the answer choices. It can be tempting to read the explanation and think that you now have a good understanding of the concept. However, an explanation likely only covers part of the question's broader context. Even if the explanation makes perfect sense, **go back and investigate** every concept related to the question until you're positive you have a thorough understanding.

As you go along, keep in mind that the practice test is just that: practice. Memorizing these questions and answers will not be very helpful on the actual test because it is unlikely to have any of the same exact questions. If you only know the right answers to the sample questions, you won't be prepared for the real thing. **Study the concepts** until you understand them fully, and then you'll be able to answer any question that shows up on the test.

It's important to wait on the practice tests until you're ready. If you take a test on your first day of study, you may be overwhelmed by the amount of material covered and how much you need to learn. Work up to it gradually.

On test day, you'll need to be prepared for answering questions, managing your time, and using the test-taking strategies you've learned. It's a lot to balance, like a mental marathon that will have a big impact on your future. Like training for a marathon, you'll need to start slowly and work your way up. When test day arrives, you'll be ready.

Start with the strategies you've read in the first two Secret Keys—plan your course and study in the way that works best for you. If you have time, consider using multiple study resources to get different approaches to the same concepts. It can be helpful to see difficult concepts from more than one angle. Then find a good source for practice tests. Many times, the test website will suggest potential study resources or provide sample tests.

4

Practice Test Strategy

If you're able to find at least three practice tests, we recommend this strategy:

UNTIMED AND OPEN-BOOK PRACTICE

Take the first test with no time constraints and with your notes and study guide handy. Take your time and focus on applying the strategies you've learned.

TIMED AND OPEN-BOOK PRACTICE

Take the second practice test open-book as well, but set a timer and practice pacing yourself to finish in time.

TIMED AND CLOSED-BOOK PRACTICE

Take any other practice tests as if it were test day. Set a timer and put away your study materials. Sit at a table or desk in a quiet room, imagine yourself at the testing center, and answer questions as quickly and accurately as possible.

Keep repeating timed and closed-book tests on a regular basis until you run out of practice tests or it's time for the actual test. Your mind will be ready for the schedule and stress of test day, and you'll be able to focus on recalling the material you've learned.

Secret Key #4 – Pace Yourself

Once you're fully prepared for the material on the test, your biggest challenge on test day will be managing your time. Just knowing that the clock is ticking can make you panic even if you have plenty of time left. Work on pacing yourself so you can build confidence against the time constraints of the exam. Pacing is a difficult skill to master, especially in a high-pressure environment, so **practice is vital**.

Set time expectations for your pace based on how much time is available. For example, if a section has 60 questions and the time limit is 30 minutes, you know you have to average 30 seconds or less per question in order to answer them all. Although 30 seconds is the hard limit, set 25 seconds per question as your goal, so you reserve extra time to spend on harder questions. When you budget extra time for the harder questions, you no longer have any reason to stress when those questions take longer to answer.

Don't let this time expectation distract you from working through the test at a calm, steady pace, but keep it in mind so you don't spend too much time on any one question. Recognize that taking extra time on one question you don't understand may keep you from answering two that you do understand later in the test. If your time limit for a question is up and you're still not sure of the answer, mark it and move on, and come back to it later if the time and the test format allow. If the testing format doesn't allow you to return to earlier questions, just make an educated guess; then put it out of your mind and move on.

On the easier questions, be careful not to rush. It may seem wise to hurry through them so you have more time for the challenging ones, but it's not worth missing one if you know the concept and just didn't take the time to read the question fully. Work efficiently but make sure you understand the question and have looked at all of the answer choices, since more than one may seem right at first.

Even if you're paying attention to the time, you may find yourself a little behind at some point. You should speed up to get back on track, but do so wisely. Don't panic; just take a few seconds less on each question until you're caught up. Don't guess without thinking, but do look through the answer choices and eliminate any you know are wrong. If you can get down to two choices, it is often worthwhile to guess from those. Once you've chosen an answer, move on and don't dwell on any that you skipped or had to hurry through. If a question was taking too long, chances are it was one of the harder ones, so you weren't as likely to get it right anyway.

On the other hand, if you find yourself getting ahead of schedule, it may be beneficial to slow down a little. The more quickly you work, the more likely you are to make a careless mistake that will affect your score. You've budgeted time for each question, so don't be afraid to spend that time. Practice an efficient but careful pace to get the most out of the time you have.

Secret Key #5 – Have a Plan for Guessing

When you're taking the test, you may find yourself stuck on a question. Some of the answer choices seem better than others, but you don't see the one answer choice that is obviously correct. What do you do?

The scenario described above is very common, yet most test takers have not effectively prepared for it. Developing and practicing a plan for guessing may be one of the single most effective uses of your time as you get ready for the exam.

In developing your plan for guessing, there are three questions to address:

- When should you start the guessing process?
- How should you narrow down the choices?
- Which answer should you choose?

When to Start the Guessing Process

Unless your plan for guessing is to select C every time (which, despite its merits, is not what we recommend), you need to leave yourself enough time to apply your answer elimination strategies. Since you have a limited amount of time for each question, that means that if you're going to give yourself the best shot at guessing correctly, you have to decide quickly whether or not you will guess.

Of course, the best-case scenario is that you don't have to guess at all, so first, see if you can answer the question based on your knowledge of the subject and basic reasoning skills. Focus on the key words in the question and try to jog your memory of related topics. Give yourself a chance to bring the knowledge to mind, but once you realize that you don't have (or you can't access) the knowledge you need to answer the question, it's time to start the guessing process.

It's almost always better to start the guessing process too early than too late. It only takes a few seconds to remember something and answer the question from knowledge. Carefully eliminating wrong answer choices takes longer. Plus, going through the process of eliminating answer choices can actually help jog your memory.

Summary: Start the guessing process as soon as you decide that you can't answer the question based on your knowledge.

7

How to Narrow Down the Choices

The next chapter in this book (**Test-Taking Strategies**) includes a wide range of strategies for how to approach questions and how to look for answer choices to eliminate. You will definitely want to read those carefully, practice them, and figure out which ones work best for you. Here though, we're going to address a mindset rather than a particular strategy.

Your odds of guessing an answer correctly depend on how many options you are choosing from.

Number of options left	5	4	3	2	1
Odds of guessing correctly	20%	25%	33%	50%	100%

You can see from this chart just how valuable it is to be able to eliminate incorrect answers and make an educated guess, but there are two things that many test takers do that cause them to miss out on the benefits of guessing:

- Accidentally eliminating the correct answer
- Selecting an answer based on an impression

We'll look at the first one here, and the second one in the next section.

To avoid accidentally eliminating the correct answer, we recommend a thought exercise called **the $5 challenge**. In this challenge, you only eliminate an answer choice from contention if you are willing to bet $5 on it being wrong. Why $5? Five dollars is a small but not insignificant amount of money. It's an amount you could afford to lose but wouldn't want to throw away. And while losing

$5 once might not hurt too much, doing it twenty times will set you back $100. In the same way, each small decision you make—eliminating a choice here, guessing on a question there—won't by itself impact your score very much, but when you put them all together, they can make a big difference. By holding each answer choice elimination decision to a higher standard, you can reduce the risk of accidentally eliminating the correct answer.

The $5 challenge can also be applied in a positive sense: If you are willing to bet $5 that an answer choice *is* correct, go ahead and mark it as correct.

Summary: Only eliminate an answer choice if you are willing to bet $5 that it is wrong.

8

Which Answer to Choose

You're taking the test. You've run into a hard question and decided you'll have to guess. You've eliminated all the answer choices you're willing to bet $5 on. Now you have to pick an answer. Why do we even need to talk about this? Why can't you just pick whichever one you feel like when the time comes?

The answer to these questions is that if you don't come into the test with a plan, you'll rely on your impression to select an answer choice, and if you do that, you risk falling into a trap. The test writers know that everyone who takes their test will be guessing on some of the questions, so they intentionally write wrong answer choices to seem plausible. You still have to pick an answer though, and if the wrong answer choices are designed to look right, how can you ever be sure that you're not falling for their trap? The best solution we've found to this dilemma is to take the decision out of your hands entirely. Here is the process we recommend:

Once you've eliminated any choices that you are confident (willing to bet $5) are wrong, select the first remaining choice as your answer.

Whether you choose to select the first remaining choice, the second, or the last, the important thing is that you use some preselected standard. Using this approach guarantees that you will not be enticed into selecting an answer choice that looks right, because you are not basing your decision on how the answer choices look.

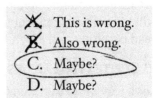

This is not meant to make you question your knowledge. Instead, it is to help you recognize the difference between your knowledge and your impressions. There's a huge difference between thinking an answer is right because of what you know, and thinking an answer is right because it looks or sounds like it should be right.

Summary: To ensure that your selection is appropriately random, make a predetermined selection from among all answer choices you have not eliminated.

Test-Taking Strategies

This section contains a list of test-taking strategies that you may find helpful as you work through the test. By taking what you know and applying logical thought, you can maximize your chances of answering any question correctly!

It is very important to realize that every question is different and every person is different: no single strategy will work on every question, and no single strategy will work for every person. That's why we've included all of them here, so you can try them out and determine which ones work best for different types of questions and which ones work best for you.

Question Strategies

⊘ READ CAREFULLY

Read the question and the answer choices carefully. Don't miss the question because you misread the terms. You have plenty of time to read each question thoroughly and make sure you understand what is being asked. Yet a happy medium must be attained, so don't waste too much time. You must read carefully and efficiently.

⊘ CONTEXTUAL CLUES

Look for contextual clues. If the question includes a word you are not familiar with, look at the immediate context for some indication of what the word might mean. Contextual clues can often give you all the information you need to decipher the meaning of an unfamiliar word. Even if you can't determine the meaning, you may be able to narrow down the possibilities enough to make a solid guess at the answer to the question.

⊘ PREFIXES

If you're having trouble with a word in the question or answer choices, try dissecting it. Take advantage of every clue that the word might include. Prefixes and suffixes can be a huge help. Usually, they allow you to determine a basic meaning. *Pre-* means before, *post-* means after, *pro-* is positive, *de-* is negative. From prefixes and suffixes, you can get an idea of the general meaning of the word and try to put it into context.

⊘ HEDGE WORDS

Watch out for critical hedge words, such as *likely, may, can, sometimes, often, almost, mostly, usually, generally, rarely,* and *sometimes*. Question writers insert these hedge phrases to cover every possibility. Often an answer choice will be wrong simply because it leaves no room for exception. Be on guard for answer choices that have definitive words such as *exactly* and *always*.

⊘ SWITCHBACK WORDS

Stay alert for *switchbacks*. These are the words and phrases frequently used to alert you to shifts in thought. The most common switchback words are *but, although,* and *however*. Others include *nevertheless, on the other hand, even though, while, in spite of, despite,* and *regardless of*. Switchback words are important to catch because they can change the direction of the question or an answer choice.

10

⊘ FACE VALUE

When in doubt, use common sense. Accept the situation in the problem at face value. Don't read too much into it. These problems will not require you to make wild assumptions. If you have to go beyond creativity and warp time or space in order to have an answer choice fit the question, then you should move on and consider the other answer choices. These are normal problems rooted in reality. The applicable relationship or explanation may not be readily apparent, but it is there for you to figure out. Use your common sense to interpret anything that isn't clear.

Answer Choice Strategies

⊘ ANSWER SELECTION

The most thorough way to pick an answer choice is to identify and eliminate wrong answers until only one is left, then confirm it is the correct answer. Sometimes an answer choice may immediately seem right, but be careful. The test writers will usually put more than one reasonable answer choice on each question, so take a second to read all of them and make sure that the other choices are not equally obvious. As long as you have time left, it is better to read every answer choice than to pick the first one that looks right without checking the others.

⊘ ANSWER CHOICE FAMILIES

An answer choice family consists of two (in rare cases, three) answer choices that are very similar in construction and cannot all be true at the same time. If you see two answer choices that are direct opposites or parallels, one of them is usually the correct answer. For instance, if one answer choice says that quantity x increases and another either says that quantity x decreases (opposite) or says that quantity y increases (parallel), then those answer choices would fall into the same family. An answer choice that doesn't match the construction of the answer choice family is more likely to be incorrect. Most questions will not have answer choice families, but when they do appear, you should be prepared to recognize them.

⊘ ELIMINATE ANSWERS

Eliminate answer choices as soon as you realize they are wrong, but make sure you consider all possibilities. If you are eliminating answer choices and realize that the last one you are left with is also wrong, don't panic. Start over and consider each choice again. There may be something you missed the first time that you will realize on the second pass.

⊘ AVOID FACT TRAPS

Don't be distracted by an answer choice that is factually true but doesn't answer the question. You are looking for the choice that answers the question. Stay focused on what the question is asking for so you don't accidentally pick an answer that is true but incorrect. Always go back to the question and make sure the answer choice you've selected actually answers the question and is not merely a true statement.

⊘ EXTREME STATEMENTS

In general, you should avoid answers that put forth extreme actions as standard practice or proclaim controversial ideas as established fact. An answer choice that states the "process should be used in certain situations, if..." is much more likely to be correct than one that states the "process should be discontinued completely." The first is a calm rational statement and doesn't even make a definitive, uncompromising stance, using a hedge word *if* to provide wiggle room, whereas the second choice is far more extreme.

⊘ BENCHMARK

As you read through the answer choices and you come across one that seems to answer the question well, mentally select that answer choice. This is not your final answer, but it's the one that will help you evaluate the other answer choices. The one that you selected is your benchmark or standard for judging each of the other answer choices. Every other answer choice must be compared to your benchmark. That choice is correct until proven otherwise by another answer choice beating it. If you find a better answer, then that one becomes your new benchmark. Once you've decided that no other choice answers the question as well as your benchmark, you have your final answer.

⊘ PREDICT THE ANSWER

Before you even start looking at the answer choices, it is often best to try to predict the answer. When you come up with the answer on your own, it is easier to avoid distractions and traps because you will know exactly what to look for. The right answer choice is unlikely to be word-for-word what you came up with, but it should be a close match. Even if you are confident that you have the right answer, you should still take the time to read each option before moving on.

General Strategies

⊘ TOUGH QUESTIONS

If you are stumped on a problem or it appears too hard or too difficult, don't waste time. Move on! Remember though, if you can quickly check for obviously incorrect answer choices, your chances of guessing correctly are greatly improved. Before you completely give up, at least try to knock out a couple of possible answers. Eliminate what you can and then guess at the remaining answer choices before moving on.

⊘ CHECK YOUR WORK

Since you will probably not know every term listed and the answer to every question, it is important that you get credit for the ones that you do know. Don't miss any questions through careless mistakes. If at all possible, try to take a second to look back over your answer selection and make sure you've selected the correct answer choice and haven't made a costly careless mistake (such as marking an answer choice that you didn't mean to mark). This quick double check should more than pay for itself in caught mistakes for the time it costs.

⊘ PACE YOURSELF

It's easy to be overwhelmed when you're looking at a page full of questions; your mind is confused and full of random thoughts, and the clock is ticking down faster than you would like. Calm down and maintain the pace that you have set for yourself. Especially as you get down to the last few minutes of the test, don't let the small numbers on the clock make you panic. As long as you are on track by monitoring your pace, you are guaranteed to have time for each question.

⊘ DON'T RUSH

It is very easy to make errors when you are in a hurry. Maintaining a fast pace in answering questions is pointless if it makes you miss questions that you would have gotten right otherwise. Test writers like to include distracting information and wrong answers that seem right. Taking a little extra time to avoid careless mistakes can make all the difference in your test score. Find a pace that allows you to be confident in the answers that you select.

⊘ KEEP MOVING

Panicking will not help you pass the test, so do your best to stay calm and keep moving. Taking deep breaths and going through the answer elimination steps you practiced can help to break through a stress barrier and keep your pace.

Final Notes

The combination of a solid foundation of content knowledge and the confidence that comes from practicing your plan for applying that knowledge is the key to maximizing your performance on test day. As your foundation of content knowledge is built up and strengthened, you'll find that the strategies included in this chapter become more and more effective in helping you quickly sift through the distractions and traps of the test to isolate the correct answer.

Now that you're preparing to move forward into the test content chapters of this book, be sure to keep your goal in mind. As you read, think about how you will be able to apply this information on the test. If you've already seen sample questions for the test and you have an idea of the question format and style, try to come up with questions of your own that you can answer based on what you're reading. This will give you valuable practice applying your knowledge in the same ways you can expect to on test day.

Good luck and good studying!

14

Types of Life Policies

Term Life Policies

There are two main types of life insurance: term life insurance and permanent life insurance. Term life insurance lasts for a specific amount of time, whereas permanent life insurance lasts for a person's whole life. **Term life insurance** only provides coverage for a designated amount of time, generally 10-30 years, which keeps premiums much lower compared to permanent life policies. Term policies do not build cash value and are designed strictly to provide a death benefit. The most common type is **level term life insurance** in which the premiums stay level, and the death benefit doesn't change. When a policy ends the insured usually has the option to renew, let it end, or possibly convert it to permanent life insurance.

INCREASING, DECREASING, AND RETURN OF PREMIUM TERM LIFE

Increasing term life insurance has a death benefit that increases each year. It usually increases either by a certain percentage or a flat rate. Since the death benefit increases, the premiums cost more than level term life insurance, and the premiums can get more expensive throughout the years. Another type of term life insurance is **decreasing term insurance** in which premiums stay the same, but the death benefit decreases at a preset and steady rate. The philosophy behind this type is that a person's need for high levels of insurance lessen as he or she gets older as certain financial obligations lessen or get resolved, such as paying off a mortgage or student loans.

Another term life insurance type is **return of premium**. These policies provide a return on the premiums paid by the insured if the term ends without a death benefit being paid out. Thus, if the insured outlives the policy, he or she will receive the premiums back from the insurer. These policies have much higher premiums because of the guarantee of the return of the insured's entire premium. Generally, the insured must not cancel the policy to get the return.

RENEWABLE AND ANNUALLY RENEWABLE TERM LIFE

Many term life insurance policies are described as being **renewable**. This is a clause that allows the policy to be renewed for another term period without the insured having to show that he or she is still in good health. If the insured continues to pay the premium, the policy will automatically renew for another term period subject to a maximum age limit, but the premiums will most likely be higher. A downside is that, depending on the policy, the premiums may only be guaranteed for one year at a time. The insurer may raise the insured's premiums every year even though it may not cancel the policy for a defined period of years.

Annually renewable term life insurance is usually less beneficial for the policyholder than for the insurer. But if the insured chooses term life insurance in an annual renewable policy, a benefit is that he or she can renew coverage each year without filling out a new application or needing to pass a physical exam. This allows the policyholder to avoid having to be re-evaluated for medical issues that have may have arisen since the initial policy institution.

Convertible Term Life

Term life policies sometimes include a provision that allows them to be **guaranteed convertible**. This provision allows the insured policyholders to change a term policy to a whole life or universal life without the need to take another physical exam or other qualifying medical tests. As long as the insured has made all the required payments, the policy can be converted. When the policy is converted, the premiums will increase. Also, the premiums before the conversion will be higher than a term life insurance policy that doesn't include the ability to convert it. Lastly, most convertible term life policies will have a deadline by which the insured will have to decide if he or she wants to convert the policy.

Permanent Life Policies

Traditional Whole Life Policies

The most popular type of **permanent life insurance** is called **whole life insurance** or **straight life insurance**. Besides the policy length of term and permanent life insurance, the other major difference between them is that permanent life insurance has something called a **cash value**. The cash value is essentially like a savings account that earns tax-deferred interest throughout the duration of the policy. The accrued cash value depends on the type of permanent life insurance policy and the established interest rate set by the insurer. In certain policies, the insured can also take out a loan from the cash value, or the cash value can offset the cost of premiums.

When an insured has whole life insurance, the **death benefit** level is steady over the insured's lifetime, so if the policy has a value of $1,000,000, the beneficiaries will receive that same monetary amount. There are a few exceptions in which the beneficiaries might not receive the full death benefit. One is if the insured dies during the **contestability period**, which is usually the first one to two years of the policy. The insurer can investigate the insured for fraud on the application and possibly deny or reduce the death benefit. Regarding suicide, most life insurance policies have a suicide clause that lasts the first two years of the policy. If the insured dies by suicide during that time, the death benefit paid to the beneficiary is only equal to the amount of premiums paid up to the time of the insured's death.

Limited Pay and Single Premium

For those insureds who desire to only pay life insurance premiums for a limited amount of time, **limited payment whole life insurance** is an option that delivers a lifetime of protection but requires only a limited number of premium payments. Since the premium payment period is limited, the policy premiums are usually much higher under this type policy. Rather than having to pay premiums for essentially most of his or her adult life, the insured can pay off the policy in just 10 or 20 years with this arrangement. Insurers also often offer limited payment plans based on age, such as the insured having to pay the premium only up to age 65.

In contrast, a **single premium whole life (SPL) policy** is, as its name implies, a whole life insurance plan with one large premium payment due at the time of issuance. The policy is fully paid up, and no further premiums are needed after that initial large payment. The SPL is fully guaranteed to remain paid up until the insured's death. A single premium whole life policy can also be referred to as a **modified endowment contract (MEC)**. There are different laws regarding how withdrawals from the cash value in MECs are taxed versus every other type of permanent life insurance policy.

Market-Sensitive/Adjustable Whole Life Policies

Variable Whole Life

Variable whole life differs from traditional whole life in that the cash value is invested in various investment accounts picked by the insurance company, such as mutual funds, annuities, money market funds, etc. This differs from the low interest rate applied to the cash value in a traditional whole life policy that the insurer picks and is only altered annually. Variable whole life policies are riskier because the policy's cash value and death benefits can rise and fall depending on market forces and the investment's performance. If the policy's investments perform well, the death benefit and cash value are likely to increase, but if the market isn't very strong, then both the death benefit and cash value can decrease. However, there is a minimum guaranteed payout to the beneficiaries if the death benefit were to lose a lot of value. Because of the investment aspect, variable policies are considered a **security**. This means they are subject to federal securities laws, and an accompanying prospectus is required when they are sold.

Universal Life

Universal life policies differ from whole life insurance policies in that they allow the insured to alter how much he or she pays in premiums and alter the death benefit for his or her beneficiaries. An insured can pay less money in premiums or skip some premium payments if he or she has enough money in the cash value to cover the difference. There are also different types of universal life policies that invest the cash value in different ways.

Variable Universal Life

This type of life insurance combines variable whole life and universal life. Like in variable whole life, the cash value is invested in various accounts, and like in universal life, the insured has the flexibility to alter their premium payments and the death benefit. Variable universal life insurance policies, along with normal variable life policies, allow an insured to have options to consider in choosing whether the death benefit will consist of strictly the original death benefit amount or will increase by the cash value or the amount of the premiums paid. The policy premiums and/or fees will vary based on which option is selected.

Interest-Sensitive Whole Life and Equity-Indexed Universal Life

Interest-sensitive whole life is often known as either **excess interest** or **current assumption** whole life. These policies provide facets of both traditional whole life with universal life features. Instead of using dividends to gain improved cash value, the interest gained on the policy's cash value is tied to the stock market and fluctuates in alignment with current market conditions. The indices used for this purpose most frequently are the **consumer price index (CPI)** or **S&P 500**. As with a whole life policy, death benefits with these policies also stays constant for life, but policy premium payments can vary.

The insurer creates expectations regarding the insured's policy related to investment gains, mortality, and expenses. If the company is successful and makes good estimates of performance, then the policy functions as the insurer hoped. But then if the market climbs and the company does well as a result, the insured's premiums will lessen, and the policy's cash value will go up.

In contrast, **equity-indexed universal life insurance** has the same features as traditional universal life insurance, but it offers insureds the ability to put their cash value in an account that pays interest according to the performance of a stock market index. These policies offer growth potential without the risks that accompany actually investing in the equities market.

Equity-indexed life insurance, as with other permanent life insurance policies, generally offers policyholders three unique tax advantages all within one life insurance product. These tax advantages include:

- Tax-deferred accumulation of cash values
- Potential for tax-managed income for retirement or other goals
- Tax-free proceeds transferable at death

PREEXISTING CONDITIONS

Preexisting conditions are no longer an impediment for applicants considering the purchase of life insurance. This is true particularly if the insured shows that the condition or illness is under control with medication or that it is in remission. For example, depending on the insurer, a man whose skin cancer was caught at an early stage might be eligible for life insurance once he is in remission for a period of time. It is possible the insured may pay a higher premium than an individual without a serious preexisting condition, but an applicant is less likely than in years past to be rejected outright.

Annuities

An annuity is a type of contract you can purchase from an insurance company or financial services company that states that the company will pay you in fixed installments in the future. It is often used for retirement. The funds that the buyer gives the company earn interest, usually on a tax-deferred basis. There are various types of annuities that alter these general aspects.

IMMEDIATE AND DEFERRED ANNUITIES

There are two general types of annuities, which differ based on when their payouts start. An **immediate annuity** is set up to give annuitants guaranteed income almost instantly after it is purchased. This is in contrast to a **deferred annuity,** which pays out fixed income to the annuitant at a later date that is stated in the contract. In each type, how big the payments are, how often they come, and how long they last are all features agreed upon before the contract is signed. In an immediate annuity, the annuitant makes one lump-sum payment. It is also called a **single-premium immediate annuity (SPIA)**. In a **deferred annuity**, the annuitant can pay either one lump sum, known as a **single-premium deferred annuity (SPDA),** or in installments over a set period, known as a **flexible premium annuity**. Regardless of which one is chosen, deferred annuities have two stages. The first is the **savings phase (or accumulation phase)**, in which the annuity holder invests funds into the account by paying their premiums, and those funds earn interest. Second is the **income phase (or payout phase)**, which is when the plan starts its payments to the annuitant.

FLEXIBLE PREMIUM ANNUITY

Flexible premium annuities grant annuitants access to **retirement funding** with flexible terms regarding how they add to the annuity. These annuities are **tax-deferred**, helping policyholders develop savings toward retirement, maximizing their contributions up front. The annuitant can change the amount and occurrence of payments to fund the annuity as he or she chooses. The annuity includes a **savings account** that credits higher interest rates to gain higher balances. The savings feature does not guarantee a policyholder a defined return on investment, however. Instead, the value fluctuates while interest and investment earnings develop on a tax-deferred basis. Flexible premium annuities usually do not include surrender or withdrawal fees. However, because contributions are tax-free, withdrawals of the tax-deferred interest and gains are **taxed** in compliance with the annuitant's ordinary income tax rate at the time of withdrawal.

STANDARD FEES THAT APPLY TO ANNUITY PRODUCTS

Annuities often have attached fees or charges that annuitants need to understand very well. These fees include insurance charges, surrender charges, investment management fees, and rider charges.

- **Insurance charges** are sometimes referred to as mortality and expense (M&E) fees and administrative fees. These charges are generally 0.5-1.5% annually.
- **Surrender charges** are included by insurance companies to limit the number of withdrawals an annuitant can take over a set number of years from the beginning of the annuity. To do this, insurers may include a surrender charge on any withdrawals above an established threshold. These charges provide assurance to the insurer that it will receive some income if an annuitant decides to end or alter the policy.
- **Investment coordination fees** are added depending on the investment choices made within the annuity product.

ILLIQUID ANNUITIES

Deposits into annuity contracts are typically untouchable for a designated period and are not able to be accessed. That means an annuity is viewed as being the opposite of a liquid asset, or rather **illiquid**. Annuities vary widely in how liquid they are as far as their ability to be converted to cash. If funds are withdrawn earlier than stipulated in the annuity contract, in the period known as the **surrender period**, the annuitant would need to pay a penalty. These surrender periods can last anywhere from two to more than 10 years, depending on the specificity in the contract. Surrender fees generally begin at 10 percent of the annuity's value, and then the penalty typically lessens annually over the surrender period. There is also an early withdrawal penalty of 10 percent charged by the IRS for withdrawing funds from the annuity if the annuitant is under the age of 59 and one-half.

VESTING

The term vesting applies to annuities when an annuitant decides to withdraw the entire balance before the end of the term as defined in the contract. Vesting refers to the annuitant gaining ownership of a certain percentage of the annuity that then cannot be denied to them. The annuity contract may state how long the **vesting period** is. Some annuities will credit zero or only part of an index-linked interest paid out to the annuitant. The percentage that is vested generally increases on a graduated scale as time advances toward the end of the term. At the term's end, an annuities vesting will be 100 percent. For instance, an annuity with a four-year term might be vested at 25 percent, 50 percent, 75 percent, and 100 percent at the end of each year.

FIXED AND VARIABLE ANNUITIES

Two standard types of annuities are variable and fixed. These refer to the type of interest that the annuitant gets on his or her account. **Variable annuities** involve greater investment risk because they do not offer a guaranteed minimum interest rate. The money in a variable annuity is invested in various funds, and thus the rate of return depends on market performance. **Fixed annuities** are safer because they provide a guaranteed minimum rate of return that is not impacted by fluctuations in market forces or the company's yearly profits. The insurer provides a specific credited rate of return using the financial performance seen in its general account funds. They do not provide the opportunity for more financial gain like in a variable annuity, but they don't come with the same risk.

INDEXED ANNUITY

An indexed annuity differs from a fixed or variable annuity because its investment returns are based on the performance of a specific stock index. Some policies provide a guaranteed rate for

lifetime income through optional riders. An element of indexed annuities that can be confusing to annuitants is how investment returns are calculated. To determine how the insurance company calculates the return, understanding how the insurer tracks the stock index it uses is helpful. Annuitants also need to know how much of the return of the index is credited to the insured.

JOINT LIFE ANNUITY (JOINT AND SURVIVOR ANNUITY)

A joint life annuity (also known as a joint and survivor annuity) pays income for the lifetime of two people, typically a married couple. In a joint life annuity, a set payment is made to the annuitants each month. After the death of one annuitant, the monthly payments continue to be made to the surviving annuitant but are typically reduce by a predetermined amount, often 50%. When the second annuitant dies, the monthly payments cease.

A joint life annuity may include a **period certain** provision, in which monthly payments continue to be made for a stated length of time even if both annuitants die before the period has elapsed. For example, a joint life annuity with 20 years certain guarantees that monthly payments will be made for a minimum of 20 years. If both annuitants die before the 20th year has elapsed, the payments will be made to an identified beneficiary until the end of the 20th year. If at least one annuitant survives beyond the guarantee period, the monthly payments will cease upon the death of the final annuitant.

Types of Life Policies Chapter Quiz

1. Which of the following is based on the philosophy that a person's need for high levels of insurance lessens as they get older and certain financial obligations lessen or get resolved?

   a. Convertible term life insurance
   b. Increasing term life insurance
   c. Decreasing term life insurance
   d. Return of premium term life insurance

2. What is another way to refer to a single premium whole life (SPL) policy?

   a. Limited payment whole life (LPL) policy
   b. Modified endowment contract (MEC)
   c. Consumer price index (CPI) policy
   d. Single-premium extension plan (SPEP)

3. Which of the following is considered a security, and is subject to federal securities laws?

   a. Variable policies
   b. Traditional policies
   c. Universal policies
   d. Equity-index policies

4. What fee or charge often attached to annuities is included by insurance companies to limit the number of withdrawals an annuitant can take over a set number of years from the beginning of the annuity?

   a. Rider charges
   b. Insurance charges
   c. Surrender charges
   d. Investment management fees

5. When an annuity contract is untouchable for a designated period and not accessible, it is:

   a. Joint
   b. Fixed
   c. Vesting
   d. Illiquid

Life Policy Riders, Provisions, Options, and Exclusions

WAIVER OF PREMIUM RIDER

A **rider** attaches added coverage to a life insurance policy over and above the simple death benefit as defined by the standard policy. Riders can either provide a free added benefit or, for an additional cost, be added to the base policy. A **waiver of premium** rider allows an insured to have his or her life insurance premiums forgiven if the insured incurs a disability that limits his or her ability to earn a living. Without this rider, the inability to pay the insurance premium could lead to cancellation of the coverage. The premiums are waived for the length of the disability. Some insurers also allow insureds who develop a disability and who have the added waiver of premium rider to convert their term policies into permanent insurance policies.

GUARANTEED INSURABILITY RIDER

A **guaranteed insurability rider** in a life insurance policy, gives policyholders the opportunity to buy additional life insurance without additional **underwriting** and **medical screening**. With the guaranteed insurability rider, a policyholder can choose when to add to the policy's death benefit without the need to provide any proof of good health or insurability and without the need to take a medical exam.

PAYER BENEFIT PROVISION

A provision that is most often found in children's life insurance policies is the **payer benefit provision**. This provision provides that premiums will be suspended if the person responsible for paying the insurance premiums, often the child's parent or guardian, becomes disabled or dies before the child reaches adulthood. If this occurs, premiums are waived.

ACCIDENTAL DEATH AND DISMEMBERMENT

Accidental death and dismemberment (AD&D) insurance provides coverage for policyholders that experience serious bodily harm or death caused by an accident. Therefore, AD&D coverage is limited in scope with a lump-sum payout benefit in the event of either an accidental death, loss of body parts (e.g., leg, arm, hand), or loss of functions (e.g., eyesight, hearing). It does not cover illnesses.

Loss of body members usually refers to a limb that has been severed from the body; however, it can also mean the loss of an insured's hands or feet or the loss of sight in one or both eyes. It can also include the general loss of use of the limb as well. Usually the AD&D benefits are payable no matter where the injury occurred, including while at work. Hospital, surgical, and other medical expenses are not generally covered by AD&D policies. Some AD&D policies provide a partial benefit if the insured loses one limb or eyesight in one eye.

AD&D coverage is made available in a variety of ways. It can be part of an individual disability income policy, a life insurance policy rider, or it can be purchased as a single policy. AD&D coverage can also be purchased or obtained as part of a group life or group health plan as a rider benefit for an additional fee.

A common way to purchase AD&D coverage is through an offering from a credit card company. Frequently these companies provide a small amount of AD&D coverage, say $1,000, without charge or for a limited time, and offer the opportunity to increase this amount for a small premium added to each month's credit card statement.

Accidental death and dismemberment insurance policies are usually purchased as riders for life insurance or health insurance. In the case of life insurance, the AD&D rider provides a separate, additional benefit if the policyholder's death occurs due to an accident, often doubling the amount of the life insurance payout. Accidental death benefits are not paid for all accidental deaths; there are some notable exclusions for inherently dangerous activities, such as a death that is the result of military service. Death or injury due to the insured's participation in illegal activities, self-inflicted injuries, or hazardous hobbies (e.g., skydiving, rock climbing, cliff diving, etc.), are also excluded. If an insured participates in these activities, the insurer may require the insured to pay a higher premium or have the activities excluded from coverage.

TERM RIDERS

Term life riders can be added to permanent life insurance policies to provide additional coverage for a certain period, such as 10, 15, or 20 years. This rider provides an additional death benefit on top of the permanent life insurance death benefit for the period it covers. Attaching this rider to the term life policy allows the policyholder to retain the term life rider even if they convert into a permanent life insurance plan at a later time. Having portions of the life coverage be both term and permanent saves the insured premium dollars at the beginning of the policy with the option to convert the term coverage into a permanent policy later. This conversion can be accomplished without going through the underwriting process or medical exam normally associated with an application for a permanent life insurance.

Term life insurance riders can be purchased by a permanent life insurance policyholder for his or her spouse. The **spouse term insurance rider** typically provides a small death benefit if the policyholder's spouse dies within the contracted term. As a bonus, the rider may be converted into its own life insurance policy without evidence of insurability at both the spouse's attained age, as well as at various points available to the policyholder. These points include:

- Within 60 days before a rise in the policy's premium
- The end of coverage through a rider
- When the insured reaches 65 years of age

If the insured dies during the premium-paying period, the spouse's coverage carries on as paid-up term coverage, without any further premium due. Policyholders may also purchase term life insurance for their children through a rider attached to a life insurance policy. The **children's term insurance rider** is convertible as well without the child needing to undergo a medical exam or provide evidence of insurability. This is available when your child is a newborn, and it lasts up until he or she is 18 or, sometimes, 25.

LONG-TERM CARE RIDERS

Long-term care riders added to permanent life insurance allow policyholders to combine two important coverage needs and allow the opportunity for the two benefits to work together. If long-term care is needed by the policyholder in any covered facility, including assisted living and home health care, the life insurance policy can convert the coverage to provide long-term care benefits. In these circumstances, instead of a death benefit paid out to beneficiaries, **long-term care benefits** become available instead. The transfer of coverage draws down the existing life insurance death benefit. If the coverage value has not been exhausted at the point that long-term care is no longer needed, the policy will revert to its original permanent life insurance state at the reduced amount.

RETURN OF PREMIUM RIDER

Life insurance carriers began offering **return-of-premium riders** on their term policies because traditional term policies only pay benefits when the insured dies. However, if the policyholder doesn't die before the term ends, this rider lets him or her regain all or part of the premiums he or she paid to the insurer over the policy's life. It also allows the insurer to use the paid premiums as an investment during the length of the term. Including this rider makes the premiums much higher than a term life insurance without it.

ENTIRE CONTRACT PROVISION

A life insurance contract typically states that the policy and the application form are combined to become the **entire contract** agreed to between the applicant and the insurer. Therefore, the entire contract includes the application for insurance, the written policy, and any declarations, riders, insuring agreements, exclusions, conditions, and endorsements. Once the contract is completed and the policy is signed, no changes can be made by anyone, unless the policyowner makes adjustments through future riders, endorsements, or amendments.

INSURING CLAUSE PROVISION

The central component at the heart of an insurance contract is what's termed the **insuring clause provision**, which contains details on the type and specifics of coverage issued by the insurer. This clause is the linchpin of the insurance policy because it details everything a life insurance policy accomplishes in protecting the insured. The insuring clause specifies that when an insured makes his or her premium payment, the company will provide a stated amount to the beneficiary or the insured as stipulated in the policy.

FREE LOOK PROVISION

The **free look provision** provides the insured with a review period following the actual delivery of the policy. The period usually lasts about 10-30 days, and during it the insured can do additional homework and decide either to keep the policy or return it to the insurance company and receive a full refund of the premium. The free look period officially begins when the policy is physically delivered to the insured and the policyholder pays any outstanding premium. At that time, the insured signs and dates the delivery receipt and the agent serves as a witness. Obviously, the policy does provide coverage on the life of the insured during this free look period because the policy is already bound.

CONSIDERATION CLAUSE

For an insurance contract to be binding, each of the parties involved must receive **consideration**, or something of substantial value. With insurance products, the policyholder provides a premium payment to the insurer (the insurer's consideration) and the insurer gives the policyholder a policy that promises to pay a death benefit according to the terms of the policy (the policyholder's consideration). The consideration clause is the part of the contract that identifies the premium payment schedule and the designated figure to be paid for a defined level of coverage.

OWNER'S RIGHTS

An owner of a life insurance policy can exercise all policy rights and privileges without the consent of the named beneficiary. The **owner's rights** do not require agreement or the consent of the beneficiary for things such as:

- Assigning or transferring the policy
- Selecting or changing the payment schedule
- Choosing a new beneficiary (as long as the beneficiary is not irrevocable)
- Selecting settlement choices
- Having conversion options or nonforfeiture options

The policyowner may also exercise options related to dividend disbursement without consulting the beneficiary. That means policyholders may receive or borrow any cash values and/or dividends that have accrued to that point without getting permission from the beneficiary. Owner's rights also include the ability to cancel the coverage altogether without the beneficiary's consent.

PRIMARY AND CONTINGENT BENEFICIARIES

The **beneficiary** is the person whom the insured picked to receive the policy's death benefit upon the insured's death. The **primary beneficiary** is identified as the individual with the first claims to the policy proceeds upon the insured's death. However, the primary beneficiary can be multiple parties. For example, the primary beneficiary can be a spouse and a child. In that case, the death benefit will be split among the beneficiaries per the instructions left by the policyowner.

A **contingent beneficiary** is designated by the policyowner as the secondary claimant with rights to the policy proceeds. The contingency means that if the primary beneficiary predeceases the insured, then the contingency beneficiary receives the death benefit.

MAKING CHANGES IN LIFE INSURANCE POLICY BENEFICIARIES

The life insurance policy terms define the process for a policyowner to make beneficiary changes. Many life insurance plans allow the policyowner to designate new primary and/or contingent beneficiaries, as often as desired, while the policy is in force.

In most cases, the owner of the policy is also the insured. When ownership of a policy is transferred, a change in the designation of beneficiaries is not a given, so care must be taken to ensure this change happens as soon as possible. Whenever a change of a beneficiary is desired, the policyholder must contact either the agent or the insurance company to begin the process and complete the proper paperwork to document the beneficiary change.

REVOCABLE AND IRREVOCABLE BENEFICIARIES

In addition to being classified as primary and contingent, beneficiaries are also classified as **revocable and irrevocable**. When the insured is the owner of the insurance contract, he or she can name anyone as his or her beneficiary, even if the person possesses no insurable interest in the insured's life. If the person named as the beneficiary is a **revocable beneficiary**, the insured can revoke that designation as often as he or wishes and at any time. In contrast, an **irrevocable beneficiary** is one that cannot be changed unless the insured has the consent of that beneficiary.

DETERMINING BENEFICIARIES WHEN A COMMON DISASTER IMPACTS THE BENEFICIARIES OF A POLICY

When included in a policy, the **common disaster clause** provides that if the insured and the designated beneficiary die simultaneously or due to the same common event, it is assumed that the beneficiary died first. This clause is helpful to streamline the death benefit payout, as it enables the policy proceeds to be paid to the contingent beneficiary and avoids having the policy proceeds be paid to the primary beneficiary's estate. If there is no contingent beneficiary named, then the proceeds are paid directly to the insured's estate.

Another component of the common disaster clause provides that the policyholder can indicate a time period (e.g., 30 days, 90 days, etc.) by which the primary beneficiary must outlive the insured for the primary beneficiary to collect the death benefit and policy proceeds.

DETERMINING BENEFITS IF THE BENEFICIARIES ARE MINORS AT THE TIME OF THE EVENT

When a child under the age of 18 is named as a beneficiary, it is problematic since persons under age 18 cannot legally enter contracts on their own. Because of their legal standing, minors are limited in receiving funds such as a death benefit from a life insurance policy—even when designated as primary beneficiaries. If a child is named as a beneficiary, a **financial guardian** will need to be appointed by a court to administer any death benefit funds received on behalf of the minor beneficiary. In most states, the financial guardian will remain in place until the beneficiary reaches the age of majority (18 years of age in most states).

MODE OF PREMIUM PAYMENT

Premium payment schedules and payment amounts vary among insurance companies. Often insurers give policyowners multiple options as to how and when they may pay their life insurance premiums. The frequency of an insured's payments is called the **mode of premium payment**.

Depending on the insurer, the following options are available for the mode of premium payment may be allowed: annually, semiannually, quarterly, or monthly. Premium payment amounts are either:

- **Level** (as with ordinary life insurance): Usually this is a monthly, quarterly fixed, or defined payment schedule.
- **Single payment** (as with single premium whole life): The policy calls for a one-time lump sum premium payment.
- **Graded premium** (as with graded premium whole life): Premiums are set on either an increasing or decreasing payment schedule.
- **Flexible premium** (as with universal life): The insured can alter his or her premium payments as seen fit within policy guidelines, making payment options very flexible.

GRACE PERIOD

If the insured fails to make the regularly scheduled premium payment by the date specified within the policy, he or she will enter a **grace period**. During the grace period, the premium payment can be made without the possibility of the insurer terminating the insured's coverage. Typically, a 30-day grace period is standard. In the case of premiums not being received by the end of the grace period, the insurer will terminate the policy. The policy does remain in full effect for the duration of the grace period. If the insured passes away during the grace period, the face amount of the policy will be paid to the chosen beneficiary, but the insurer will deduct the amount of the premium due from the amount it pays to the beneficiary.

AUTOMATIC PREMIUM LOAN

If a policyholder misses a life insurance premium payment deadline, the policy enters the grace period. In this circumstance, an insured can call on a backup provision called an **automatic premium loan**, if available on his or her policy, to provide a stopgap measure to make the premium payment automatically. When this provision is included in a life policy, the insurer provides the premium payment on behalf of the insured. To account for this, the insurer will charge that same amount against the policy's current cash value at a standard rate stipulated in the policy. This standard rate is also used to administer other policy loans available under terms of the contract. Ultimately, the key factor is that for the provision to work, there must be cash value available within the policy.

LEVEL AND FLEXIBLE PREMIUM PAYMENT SCHEDULES

A **level premium payment** is a provision defined in the policy where each premium payment made by the insured is the exact same amount over the entire life of the contract, except for normal increases. However, when the policy is renewed, the premium level is adjusted to coincide with the insured's attained age and then, the new premium remains the same amount during that new timeframe.

The **flexible premium payment**, meanwhile, is used in flexible premium life policies and variable premium life policies. This structure allows the insured a great deal of flexibility to vary both the amount of premium he or she pays, as well as when the insured makes his or her premium payments. Whenever the change in payments is adjusted, the amount of insurance in force will also likely need an adjustment.

MAKING WITHDRAWALS FROM THE POLICY'S CASH VALUE

The term withdrawal simply means that the policyholder is taking out available funds from the life insurance policy's cash value. Withdrawals can only be made if there is adequate cash value available in the policy. If withdrawals are allowed under the policy rules, then they are usually, but not always, made tax-free up to the maximum amount allowed by per the policy. The basis withdrawal amount is the total of the premiums the policyholder has already paid for the policy, minus any earlier dividends paid to the insured and/or any previous withdrawals made by the policyholder.

REINSTATEMENT OF LIFE INSURANCE POLICIES LAPSED DUE TO NON-PAYMENT OF PREMIUM

Reinstatement is the process of reinstalling a policy that's become lapsed due to nonpayment of premiums. In most cases, permanent life insurance contracts permit policyowners to reinstate a lapsed policy. Under this reinstatement provision, the policyowner will be responsible for paying back all outstanding premiums with interest. Unless the policy has been surrendered for cash, it may be reinstated within a three-year timeframe (in most policies) after the last premium is paid prior to the policy's default. The insured will receive the protection of the original policy if the policyowner does the following:

- Presents appropriate and approved **evidence of insurability** (medical examination)
- Pays back premiums he or she owes plus interest
- Pays any other debt or policy loans owed to the insurer plus interest

A reinstated policy usually starts a new contestable period (two years); however, it does not require a new suicide period.

POLICY LOANS AND PARTIAL SURRENDERS

When an insured decides to only take a portion of the cash value from his or her life insurance policy, it is termed a **partial surrender**. In this situation, the policyowner is taking money from the policy without any plans of returning the cash to the policy.

On the other hand, when an insured takes a **policy loan** against the cash value of the life insurance policy, the interest charged on the loan is a defined rate detailed in the policy, subject to applicable state regulations. The loan may be paid back at any time; in fact, there is no set schedule for repaying the loan.

- If the interest is not paid and the loan amount increases to a level in excess of the cash value, the policy will be terminated by the insurer.
- If the insured dies after taking out a loan against the policy, the loan amount, in addition to any applicable interest, will be subtracted from the remaining balance to lessen the death benefit paid out to the beneficiary.
- If the cash value is depleted, the policy will be terminated after the insurer notifies the insured.

NONFORFEITURE OPTION

Nonforfeiture options are available in permanent insurance contracts. In an insurance policy, a **nonforfeiture provision** states that the insured may receive all or some of the benefits or a partial refund on the premiums that have already been paid in the event that the policy lapses because the insured neglects to make premium payments. Often, a nonforfeiture clause will only stay in effect for a set timeframe at the outset of the policy. The nonforfeiture clause may also only become active if the policy has been in force after a certain amount of time, per stipulations detailed in the contract.

PAYING DIVIDENDS

Permanent insurance policies often permit policyowners to draw **dividends**. When an insurer's overall investments perform well, dividends can be paid out to the policyholders. But dividends are not the same as earnings accrued from stock ownership. Dividends, being based on investment returns, are not guaranteed, just as excellent investment performance is never guaranteed. Insureds can receive dividends on many permanent policies, depending on their contract provisions and the insurer. Insurers provide dividends to their insureds in varied ways and can disperse them via cash or in dividend checks. Dividends can also be used either to add more insurance coverage or to help fund future premium costs.

AVAILABLE DIVIDEND OPTIONS

Insurers typically offer several dividend options depending on the policy. A permanent life policy for instance typically has the following dividend options:

- Purchase additional paid-up insurance with dividends
- Use dividends toward the payment of policy premiums
- Keep dividends in your account to earn interest, which will be taxable
- Repay policy loans with dividends
- Purchase a one-year term insurance benefit, if offered by the insurer

INCONTESTABILITY CLAUSE

The **incontestability clause** offers protection to the insured and generally goes into effect after a two-year period that starts on the policy's effective date. After this two-year period, the insurer can no longer question and investigate statements made in the insurance application as being fraudulent, and thus the insurer can no longer seek to suspend or contest a policyholder's coverage. If not for the incontestability clause, insurers could require insureds to confirm statements made on the application years or decades later. The clause guarantees the insured benefits when it goes into effect. If the policy were to lapse, a later reinstatement of the policy would require the beginning of a new incontestability period.

OPTION OF ASSIGNMENT

Assignment of life insurance shifts the owner's rights in a policy, in whole or in part, to another individual. There are two types of assignment: absolute assignment and collateral assignment.

- **Absolute assignment (aka total assignment)** is the transfer of the entire policy, complete with all its rights to another individual who then is the policyholder.
- In contrast, **collateral (or conditional) assignment** allows the death benefit to be used as collateral for any debt the policyowner had accrued.

Collateral assignment places a policy's death benefit with a lending organization as collateral for a loan taken by the insured. As a result, the entity receiving the collateral assignment is transferred only those policy rights that are applicable to establish collateral and balance the insured's debt.

SUICIDE PROVISIONS

Standard **suicide clauses** within life insurance policies state, depending on state insurance regulations, that if in the first one or two years of a policy's existence, an insured takes his or her own life, the company will not pay the death benefit to the beneficiary. Instead, the insurer will only pay out as a benefit the premium payments made to the insurer to that date. A suicide that occurs after the period noted in the suicide clause (usually one or two years after the policy's effective date) will result in the beneficiary getting the policy's full death benefit.

MISSTATEMENT OF AGE OR GENDER

If a deceased insured misrepresented his or her age, the face amount of the policy will be changed and reestablished to the amount that the premium would have bought at the insured's correct age at the time of purchase. The incontestability period does not apply to misstatements of age or gender. For example, if an insured claimed on the insurance application four years earlier to be 43 years old when in fact, he or she was 53 years old, the $250,000 policy purchased would be adjusted to a lower face amount in the event of his or her death. An overstatement of age will usually result in a refund of premium payment.

AVAILABLE SETTLEMENT OPTIONS

The following are standard settlement options available to life insurance beneficiaries:

- **Lump-sum cash settlement**: When receiving a lump-sum payment, the named beneficiary receives the entire policy face amount at once.
- **Interest only**: With this option the beneficiary can get an interest-only limited benefit and defer the face amount to a later time he or she selects.
- **Fixed period installments**: With this option, the death benefit is distributed as equal monthly payments for the selected period of time until the entire face amount plus accrued interest is paid.
- **Fixed amount installments**: If this option is chosen, the beneficiary will receive monthly payments in the specified amount until the entire face amount plus accrued interest is paid.
- **Life income options**: If the beneficiary selects the life income option, he or she receives the proceeds of the policy as an annuity.

ACCELERATED DEATH BENEFITS

A clause in certain life insurance policies permits insureds to receive benefits before death if there is a diagnosis of a terminal illness. The amount an insured can pull from the policy differs by policy stipulations and by the insurer. If the policyholder takes an **accelerated benefit**, the insurer then deducts that withdrawn dollar amount from the policy's death benefit that will later be paid out to the assigned beneficiary. This extra benefit option is often provided as an add-on to the insured's premium.

Accelerated death benefits are typically offered as an add-on to the following types of policies:

- Permanent life insurance
- Group permanent life insurance
- Term life insurance
- Group term life

VIATICAL SETTLEMENT

A **viatical settlement** is the sale of a policyholder's existing life insurance coverage to a private individual. Generally, the original policyowner receives less than the policy's net death benefit but receives more than the amount of its cash surrender requirement. The insured often agrees to a viatical settlement because they are terminally or chronically ill. Such a sale provides the policyowner with a lump sum payment to use as he or she wishes. Typically, the policyowner and the insured are the same person so this viatical settlement allows the insured to replace his or her lost wages, pay medical bills, or cover bills like mortgage payments. The third party that buys the life insurance policy then becomes the new owner of the policy, continues the monthly premium payments, and receives the full benefit of the policy when the insured dies.

POLICY EXCLUSIONS

Insurers restrict or exclude paying out death benefits for activities that are inherently dangerous. The most common life insurance **exclusions** are:

- **Suicide clause**
- **Dangerous activity exclusion** (e.g., cliff diving, mountaineering, auto racing, or hang gliding)
- **Aviation exclusion** (the insured piloting his or her own small airplane)
- **Act of war exclusion** (death benefits not provided if death is caused during military service or an act of war)

Other exclusions include drug or alcohol abuse and the participation in illegal activities that caused a fatal accident.

Regarding dangerous activities, some life insurers will charge applicants a higher premium if the individual regularly participates in them instead of excluding them completely. If the dangerous activity is a short-term endeavor, such as the opportunity to scuba dive the Great Barrier Reef, it might be more prudent for the insured to purchase a **short-term accidental death and dismemberment policy**.

Life Policy Riders, Provisions, Options, and Exclusions Chapter Quiz

1. A waiver of premium rider allows an insured to have their life insurance premiums forgiven if:

    a. An inability to pay the insurance premium is due to unemployment
    b. The insured incurs a disability that limits their ability to earn a living
    c. The insured has an immediate death in the family i.e., child, spouse, etc.
    d. The insured undergoes additional underwriting and medical screening

2. Accidental death and dismemberment insurance policies are usually purchased as:

    a. A single policy
    b. Credit card bonuses
    c. Part of individual disability income policies
    d. Riders for life insurance or health insurance

3. Which of the following says that if the policyholder doesn't die before the term ends, the rider will let him or her regain all or part of the premiums that were paid to the insurer over the policy's life?

    a. AD&D riders
    b. Spouse term insurance riders
    c. Return-of-premium riders
    d. Long-term care riders

4. The central component at the heart of an insurance contract is called the:

    a. Entire contract provision
    b. Insuring clause provision
    c. Consideration clause
    d. Free look provision

5. Which of the following indicates that if the insured and the designated beneficiary die simultaneously or due to the same common event, it is assumed that the beneficiary died first?

    a. Flexible provisions
    b. Grace period
    c. Free look provision
    d. Common disaster clause

6. What type of premium payment is typically a monthly, quarterly fixed, or defined payment schedule?

    a. Level
    b. Single payment
    c. Graded premium
    d. Flexible premium

7. A reinstated policy usually starts a new:

    a. Review period
    b. Contestable period
    c. Suicide period
    d. Guarantee period

8. Which of the following states that the insured may receive all or some of the benefits or a partial refund on the premiums that have already been paid in the event that their policy lapses?

a. Nonforfeiture provision
b. Partial surrender
c. Incontestability clause
d. Waiver of premium rider

9. How would the situation be rectified if a deceased insured misrepresented their age?

a. The designated beneficiary can utilize the cash value of the policy to cover the discrepancy caused by the age difference.
b. If a deceased insured misrepresented his or her age, then the policy is voided or terminated due to a misstatement of fact.
c. If the insured is within his or her incontestability period, then the beneficiary will receive the policy's full death benefit, with no adjustments.
d. The policy's face amount will change and be reestablished to the amount that the premium should have been in regard to the insured's correct age at the time of purchase.

10. What standard settlement choice means the beneficiary will receive the proceeds of the policy as an annuity?

a. Interest only
b. Fixed period installments
c. Fixed amount installments
d. Life income option

Completing the Application, Underwriting, and Delivering the Life Policy

REQUIRED SIGNATURES

For an insurance application to be accepted as complete and credible by the insurer, both the insured and the agent must sign it. Not only are the signatures required, but they also attest that the insured is verifying that all the information on the application is completely accurate and true, and the agent's signature affirms and reinforces the application. Another signature may be needed if the insured is not the applicant for the policy. In this case, the applicant (policyowner) must add his or her signature. Finally, if an examining physician's statement is a part of the application, the physician must also sign the application to affirm that the medical information that he or she provided is accurate and true. During the course of the contract, changes may be made. If changes are needed, both the insured and the agent must sign the application, essentially agreeing together that the changes made are satisfactory to both parties.

INCOMPLETE APPLICATION

Sometimes an agent will submit an incomplete application for life insurance coverage. When this occurs, the insurer will return incomplete applications to the agent for it to be completed properly. If a policy is issued with unanswered questions, the insurer must not interpret those missing answers as the insured waiving the right to answer the questions. This is important because once the policy is in force, the insurer can no longer deny coverage based on information that was missing—so catching these incomplete portions is important for the insurer.

MAKING CHANGES TO AN APPLICATION

There are two courses of action possible when a mistake is made and changes are needed on a life insurance application.

- First, the agent could have the applicant initial the change and then submit it to the insurer. The insurer may still ask for verification of the initials to ensure everything is accurate.
- Second, the agent could simply direct the insured to begin the process over with a new application.

What agents absolutely cannot do is alter the application by erasing a portion of it and then writing in a response themselves.

WARRANTIES AND REPRESENTATIONS

There are big differences between warranties and representations.

A **warranty** is an essential condition upon which the insurer and insured agree for the contract to take effect. For instance, in a life insurance application, a warranty might be that the insured guarantees that he or she is not presently terminally ill or in hospice care.

In contrast, a **representation** is not an essential condition of an insurance policy but is simply the current information provided in the application. Representations within a life insurance application are statements made by the applicant that impact the insurer's decision to offer insurance. Types of representations within an insurance application include such things as a person's date of birth, a list of current medical conditions, or prescription drugs currently used by the insured. Representations could also include other facts such as the insured's height and weight at the time of

33

the application. Still other representations would be factual answers to family health history questions, such as the ages when the insured's parents died and their causes of death.

INITIATING AN APPLICATION AND RECEIPT OF THE INITIAL PREMIUM

An essential part of an insurance agent's job is to walk applicants through the process of completing a life insurance application. First, the agent provides an exhaustive explanation of coverage options and accompanying premium amounts and assists the applicant in determining the best fit based on his or her coverage needs and financial resources. Next, the agent assists the applicant in completing the application and assures that he or she provides complete, accurate, and thorough information. When the application is complete, the agent and the applicant both sign it. The agent provides the insured a **conditional receipt** upon the applicant's payment of the first premium. This offers a window to the insurers to ultimately deny or approve the policy until it is determined if the insured meets the stands of insurability.

REPLACEMENT OF AN EXISTING POLICY WITH A NEW APPLICATION

Medical conditions change over time, and if an insured is considering replacing his or her current life insurance policy with a new policy, an important consideration is whether the insured is still insurable. In other words, has his or her health deteriorated in the interim to the point where he or she may not be accepted by an insurer due to a preexisting condition? A **replacement** is when a new policy or contract is purchased and the insured chooses to surrender, forfeit, or lapse the current policy in favor of the new one. The insured should consider his or her decision with potential surrender charges in mind when giving up the old policy. Insureds should never cancel an existing life insurance policy until the new policy is in place in case the medical exam reveals an uninsurable new illness.

NECESSARY DISCLOSURES AT THE POINT OF SALE

At the time of an applicant's completion of a life insurance application, insurers must provide a **disclosure statement**. This disclosure statement typically includes a summary of all the important details of the contract, such as premium amount, payment schedule, death benefit, any contract riders, and obligations of both parties. The disclosure statement also names the source of insurance and key personal information, identifying the insured by name, date of birth, and gender. The purpose of the disclosure statement is to provide applicants with a concise explanation of what they would be paying and what they would be receiving if they decide to purchase the insurance being offered. Life insurance companies must also disclose all information about the certification and maintenance of the policies they sell, including to what extent and for how long the insurer will maintain relevant records.

HIPAA DISCLOSURE

In the life insurance policy application process, the life insurer and agent are required to have the applicant sign a Health Insurance Portability and Accountability Act (HIPAA) disclosure acknowledgement. This disclosure informs the applicant that his or her personally identifiable health information will be protected and held strictly confidential by the insurer. The disclosure states that the insurer may only share this identifiable information with other entities appropriate to the life insurance application process. The disclosure describes to the insured how his or her medical information may be used and disclosed and how it may not be used and disclosed to internal and external parties. The disclosure further explains how the insured can acquire his or her own medical information and details how an insured can terminate the authorization in writing.

PROVISIONS OF THE USA PATRIOT ACT THAT IMPACT THE APPLICATION PROCESS

Insurance companies are susceptible to money laundering, and insurance agents, producers, and brokers play a key role in the insurance process. Thus, the **USA Patriot Act** established **anti-money laundering (AML)** requirements that require insurers and brokerages to include **employee training** on independent audits and policies to detect suspicious behavior and potential money laundering within insurance transactions.

The anti-money laundering regulations enacted as part of the USA Patriot Act apply to the following insurance-related products:

- Permanent life insurance, other than group life insurance
- Annuity contracts, other than a group annuity contract
- Any other insurance product with features of cash value or investment

ANTI-MONEY LAUNDERING REQUIREMENTS

Insurance producers and brokers who partner with financial institutions or insurers are mandated to comply with federal anti-money laundering regulations that seek to prevent having the insurance industry involved in financing terrorist activity. To avoid this risk, insurers are required to provide producers and brokers with anti-money laundering training. Federal rules require insurance companies that issue or underwrite covered products to develop and implement a written anti-money laundering program applicable to its covered products. Independent insurance agents and brokers are not required by the final rule to have separate anti-money laundering programs.

MEDICAL INFORMATION AND CONSUMER REPORTS

MIB Group, Inc. (formerly the Medical Information Bureau) has underwriting services that provide essential information on insurance applicants related to the risks they present to the insurer. Insurance companies submit underwriting information to MIB, and that information can then be accessed by other underwriters. The information is coded and used exclusively by the insurance companies that are members. The information MIB provides informs underwriters of risks associated with misrepresentations made on insurance applications, such as the case of errors or omissions. This helps insurers to process life and health insurance applications more effectively. The result is that insurers select the right applicants to insure, thereby reducing their risks.

FAIR CREDIT REPORTING ACT

The federal Fair Credit Reporting Act (FCRA) mandates that insurers provide notices to applicants when they take an adverse action using information gleaned from consumer reports about the applicant. An **adverse action** is any action taken by the insurer as a result of information presented in the consumer report that negatively affects the situation of an applicant. For example, suppose an insurer reviews an applicant's credit history to decide whether the applicant can afford the insurance premiums. If the insurer finds a poor credit score during its review and thus gives the applicant a surcharge in addition to the regular insurance premium, this is an adverse action, and the insurer must notify the applicant and give him or her a chance to dispute the information in the report.

RISK CLASSIFICATIONS

Insurers use **risk classifications** to place applicants in different categories according to their risk, which involves such things as height, weight, health status, tobacco use, and overall lifestyle choices. Typically, life insurers use several classifications from **preferred select,** for those applicants with optimum health, to **substandard,** for those applicants possessing poor health.

Standard is a category associated with average health and a normal life expectancy. Minor health issues may be present in this category, or perhaps, height-to-weight ratio is not optimum.

INSURABLE INTEREST

Before an application for life insurance can be approved, the underwriter will make sure that anyone named as a beneficiary has an **insurable interest** in the policyholder. An insurable interest exists when a beneficiary is reliant upon the insured for financial support or the beneficiary would incur substantial financial costs upon the insured's death. It is a given that family members and spouses have an insurable interest in the insured because they are generally responsible for burial expenses and estate responsibilities and rely on them financially while they are living. Unless there are no living relatives, a friend may not be considered to have an insurable interest. Business partners may also have an insurable interest in each other, and businesses can have an insurable interest in the lives of their employees, especially any key employees. The concept of insurable interest exists because life insurance is intended to provide security against the unexpected death of someone upon whom the beneficiaries financially rely.

SITUATIONS THAT LACK INSURABLE INTEREST

Stranger-originated life insurance (STOLI) is the term used when a person applying for life insurance wants to locate a new insurance policy with a beneficiary who has previously not known the insured and does not have an insurable interest in the insured. These policies are on the fringe of questionable business practices and have come under scrutiny from insurance regulators and the industry in general, as they may conflict with **state insurable interest laws**. A STOLI transaction is not intended to be insurance protection but is rather intended to be an investment mechanism for the policy owner's beneficiaries.

In **investor-originated life insurance (IOLI)**, a producer and/or investor approaches an individual who is usually a stranger to the investor. The investor has no financial ties to the individual that he or she is recruiting, and therefore, cannot adhere to the insurable interest standard that must be present in more legitimate life insurance policies. The investor trying to draft the prospect to become the insured sometimes offers him or her a small fee for use of his or her personal information. In many cases, individuals recruited to serve as the insured are in extremely poor health and may not live beyond the first year or two of the policy. After recruiting the individual, the investor facilitates the application for insurance and then names himself or herself as the policy's sole beneficiary. Both STOLI and IOLI transactions are very similar, except that IOLI arrangements always have an investor as the third party.

WHEN COVERAGE BEGINS

Generally, individual life insurance coverage begins as soon as the policy is approved by the insurer and the applicant provides the first insurance premium to the insurer. In group life insurance, employees often are delayed in their coverage being active due to a **new employee waiting period**. These can vary in duration, depending on the employer group. For example, some employers may have employee waiting periods of 30 days, 90 days, 6 months, or 12 months. Start dates may be different among dependent family members, which results in different waiting periods for each dependent's life insurance coverage.

EXPLAINING LIFE INSURANCE POLICIES TO CLIENTS

Insurance agents and brokers need to be patient and explain the details of a new insurance policy carefully to their insurance clients. Taking extra time to carefully discuss and explain complex insurance language and answer questions thoroughly during the sales process creates greater trust between the prospect and the agent. Life insurance is a complex topic with multiple policy options available to the insured. When the applicant has chosen a specific policy for which to apply, agents and brokers should ensure that the applicant is comfortable with all provisions, riders, and exclusions—and ultimately with how all these factors relate to the premium rate that is charged the client.

Completing the Application, Underwriting, and Delivering the Life Policy Chapter Quiz

1. Which of the following is not an essential condition of an insurance policy, but is simply the current information provided in an application?

    a. Warranty
    b. Prerequisite
    c. Representation
    d. Surety

2. What can be given to an applicant at the time of their first premium that offers a window to the insurers to deny or approve the policy?

    a. Certificate of insurance
    b. Replacement policy
    c. Disclosure statement
    d. Conditional receipt

3. What does HIPAA stand for?

    a. Health Insurance Permanent Answerability Act
    b. Health Insurance Portability and Accountability Act
    c. Health Insurance Progression and Advancement Act
    d. Health Insurance Payroll and Assets Act

4. Which of the following products is NOT affected by the anti-money laundering regulations enacted as part of the USA Patriot Act?

    a. Group permanent life insurance
    b. Any insurance product with cash value
    c. Any insurance product with investment features
    d. Annuity contracts, other than group annuity

5. What mandates that insurers provide notices to applicants when they take an adverse action using information gleaned from consumer reports about the applicant?

    a. HIPAA
    b. Fair Credit Reporting Act
    c. MIB Group, Inc. (formerly the Medical Information Bureau)
    d. USA Patriot Act

6. What is the term used when a person applying for life insurance wants to locate a new insurance policy with a beneficiary who has previously not known the insured and does not have an insurable interest in the insured?

    a. Unfamiliar representation inquiry
    b. Substandard insurable applicant
    c. Stranger-originated life insurance
    d. Third-party insurance application

Taxes, Retirement, and Other Life Insurance Concepts

UNDERWRITING

An **insurance underwriter's** primary job function is to evaluate the risks and exposures of potential clients by looking at their medical history and other risk factors. Underwriters decide if the individual's risk is acceptable to the insurer, how much coverage he or she should be offered, and what the best premium rate should be. Underwriters ultimately are tasked with protecting insurers from bad risks and setting premium rates so that they are sufficient to be profitable for the insurance company.

THIRD-PARTY OWNERSHIP

Third-party life insurance occurs when a policy is purchased with the intent to gain protection for another party. The policyholder (first party) seeks third-party insurance purchased from an insurance company (second party) to protect a third party (the insured). In third-party purchase agreements, the policyholder is not the same individual as the insured. As an example, if a father applies for and is issued a policy on his daughter's life, then the daughter is the insured (third party), and the father is the policyholder (first party).

CONVERSION PRIVILEGE

Many life insurance policies include a **conversion privilege clause** that provides individuals with an opportunity to transition easily to individual life insurance coverage after leaving an employer where they had group life insurance coverage. With this provision, employees can effectively change a group life insurance policy into an individual policy without undergoing a medical exam or additional underwriting. With this conversion, the insurer extends coverage based on the employee's previous approval for coverage and maintains an actively insured person rather than losing a client.

CONTRIBUTORY AND NONCONTRIBUTORY GROUP LIFE

In **noncontributory group life policies**, the full premium is provided by the employer with zero contribution required from the employees. Noncontributory insurance plans have an advantage for employees as they usually use **automatic-issue policies**. This means coverage through employers is automatic without needing to undergo a medical examination. Another advantage for noncontributory plans is the ease of administration for employers because they do not have the extra step of tracking employee contributions toward premiums.

With **contributory group life plans** the employee is not guaranteed coverage as these plans involve the underwriting process and risk assessment. An advantage for contributory plans is that the employer can usually offer better coverage than provided in noncontributory plans because of the enhanced funding levels.

POLICIES HELD IN RETIREMENT PLANS

Life insurance policies may only be held in certain types of retirement plans, such as defined-benefit and defined-contribution group plans. They are not permitted to be held in individual accounts such as an IRA. Additionally, there are regulations governing how much of the plan's contributions may be used to pay the policy premiums. This value can vary based on the type of plan and the type of life policy. For instance, if a defined-contribution plan holds a universal life policy, no more than 25% of the plan's contributions may be used to pay the premiums.

ADVANTAGES

There are two main advantages of having a life insurance policy held in a retirement account. First, the premium payments are made with tax-free dollars. (While this is a benefit, it also means that a portion of the death benefit may be counted as part of the deceased's estate for tax purposes.) The second advantage is that a policy held in a retirement plan is less likely to lapse for nonpayment since plan assets, rather than personal funds, are being used to pay the premiums.

DISADVANTAGES

An individual can only hold a life insurance policy within a plan while he or she is a participant of the plan. This means that the individual must be prepared to transfer ownership of the policy in the event of a job change, retirement, or the plan being terminated or changed in such a way that it is no longer a qualified plan. On the employer side of the equation, qualified plans are more complex and expensive to administrate.

SOLE PROPRIETORSHIP

Because the owner of a **sole proprietorship** is not a separate entity from the business, the owner possesses special needs and risks related to life insurance coverage. That's because when the business owner dies then the business dies too. Although the assets of the business can legally be transitioned to the named beneficiary upon the owner's death, the business itself must be closed. If the beneficiary wants to continue the business operations, then he or she will have to start a new business under his or her own name. This transition period can be costly. Instead, if the business owner plans carefully and buys good life insurance protection, the business can successfully survive the transfer and rebirth to the policy's named beneficiary.

KEY PERSON INSURANCE

A life insurance policy can be bought by a business or corporation to protect against a loss of income in the event of a **key employee's death**. The business or corporation purchases the policy and then receives the policy benefits if the key employee dies. Such a policy provides the corporation or business benefits related to the income and business lost because of the key employee's death. The coverage can also provide valuable peace of mind to a business's creditors who have uncertainties regarding the company's future in the case of a key employee's death. Having this insurance in place can also help to fortify the company's standing with any shareholders as well. Typically, employees that hold executive level positions (e.g., owner, CEO, CFO, president) are covered by a key life insurance policy.

SOCIAL SECURITY BENEFITS

An individual's Social Security benefit is calculated using a complex formula that gets you an amount called the **primary insurance amount (PIA)**. The PIA is how much you will receive in Social Security benefits if you elect to start receiving them at normal retirement age, which is 67 for people born in 1960 and after. A person is first eligible to start receiving benefits at 62; however, if you start receiving benefits before your normal retirement age, those benefits will not be your full PIA but a reduced amount that is determined by the Social Security Administration.

The complex formula takes an individual's earnings for each year and adjusts them for inflation. It does this by using the **average wage indexing (AWI) series** that Social Security determines annually. Once an individual's wages are indexed, a number called the **average indexed monthly earnings (AIME)** amount is calculated. This amount then undergoes further calculations to get the

PIA. Overall, an average worker's Social Security benefit amount can generally be expected to be about 40 percent of his or her average lifetime earnings.

The term **worker** applies to someone that has earned a total of at least 40 credits during his or her lifetime. Credits are earned when you work and pay Social Security taxes. You can earn up to four credits a year, so it usually takes 10 years to qualify for Social Security. Children are also eligible to receive Social Security benefits. A child can be eligible if he or she has at least one parent that is disabled, retired, or dead. He or she must also be unmarried and either below 18 years of age; or enrolled in high school full time and is age 19 or younger; or is age 18 and older but is disabled due to an occurrence before he or she turned age 22.

TAXING GROUP LIFE INSURANCE POLICY PREMIUMS, PROCEEDS, AND DIVIDENDS

In group life insurance plans where premiums are paid by the employer, employees can receive coverage up to a $50,000 death benefit without incurring any tax liability. However, if coverage exceeds a $50,000 death benefit, employees are required to treat the excess cost of the life insurance premium as income and pay taxes on it.

For death benefits, the beneficiaries are ordinarily not required to pay any state or federal income tax on proceeds from a life insurance policy. This is particularly true if the death benefit is received as a lump sum payment.

TAXING INDIVIDUAL LIFE INSURANCE POLICY PREMIUMS, PROCEEDS, AND DIVIDENDS

Premiums paid by an individual for a life insurance policy are not permitted to be deducted as an expense on an individual's income tax return.

An advantage of cash value life insurance is that there are no tax obligations for any earnings. An individual's earnings gained in the cash value policy are permitted to increase on a tax-deferred basis until the policy is cashed out. Generally, dividends are not taxed as income for the insured.

TAXING MODIFIED ENDOWMENT CONTRACTS (MEC) INSURANCE PROCEEDS, PREMIUMS, AND DIVIDENDS

One form of tax-qualified life insurance is a **modified endowment contract** (**MEC**), which receives excessive funding beyond its normal parameters. The IRS looks at life insurance policies differently when they become MECs because of the excess premium funding. When a life policy becomes an MEC, the process of taxation changes within the contract for money withdrawn, and the life insurance owner may be flagged for early withdrawals taken before he or she reaches age 59.5. When a life insurance policy becomes an MEC, it is considered by the IRS to be like a **nonqualified annuity**.

Taxes, Retirement, and Other Life Insurance Concepts Chapter Quiz

1. What is an insurance underwriter's primary job function?
   a. Provide the opportunity for clients to transition smoothly from one policy to the next
   b. Attach added coverage to a life insurance policy
   c. Evaluate the risks and exposures of potential clients
   d. Create the written policy and note any agreements, exclusions, conditions, or endorsements

2. What clause gives employees the option to effectively change a group life insurance policy into an individual policy after leaving their employer?
   a. Conversion privilege
   b. Automatic-reissue
   c. Contributory extension
   d. Transition advantage

3. An individual's Social Security benefit is calculated using a complex formula that produces an amount called the:
   a. Social Security leverage
   b. Primary insurance amount
   c. Average wage index
   d. Indexed monthly earnings

4. What is the maximum number of Social Security credits that can be earned in a year?
   a. 2
   b. 3
   c. 4
   d. 5

5. In group life insurance plans where premiums are paid by the employer, how much death benefit coverage can employees receive without incurring any tax liability?
   a. $5,000
   b. $20,000
   c. $35,000
   d. $50,000

Types of Health Policies

DISABILITY INCOME

When an individual incurs an illness or injury, an **individual disability income** insurance policy gives coverage that replaces a portion of the individual's lost income. Disability insurance will not replace the individual's entire income, but it will provide 60-80% of it. Unlike workers' compensation, which only provides coverage for illnesses and injuries related to the workplace, disability income insurance provides replacement of the insured's income for illnesses and injuries related to most circumstances.

To have income replaced under disability insurance an individual must meet either the total or partial disability definitions found in the policy. An individual meets the **total disability** criteria if he or she cannot work at any job related to his or her education, training, and experience. If an individual is prevented from doing only some of his or her essential tasks, it is termed **partial disability**.

The two important definitions related to disability income insurance are own occupation and any occupation. A policy that utilizes an insured's **own occupation** generally pays benefits if the insured cannot return to work in his or her current job, even if he or she can work somewhere else. Some policies might consider your specific field under own occupation, but it depends on the insurer and the policy. A policy that refers to **any occupation** generally would pay benefits only if the insured cannot perform any job at all that he or she is qualified for by education, training, or experience, even if it means taking a lower-paying job or a job in a completely new field of work. The latter policies are often considered the least friendly.

ATTENDING PHYSICIAN'S STATEMENT

An insured gives a statement providing details about the illness or injury when he or she files a claim under a disability income insurance policy. This provides written acknowledgement to the insurer of the individual's claim for benefits. In analyzing the claim, the insurer often seeks to verify the insured's statement regarding the illness or injury by requesting an **attending physician's statement (APS)**. This is completed by the insured's doctor and tells the insurer the circumstances surrounding the disability. The APS details the insured's medical history, health care plan, and how the disabling condition came to be.

INDEPENDENT MEDICAL EXAMINATION

An **independent medical examination (IME)** occurs when a doctor, physical therapist, chiropractor, or other health care professional who has not previously been involved in a person's care is sought by an insurer to examine the individual when he or she files a disability claim. Insurers will find an IME to garner a second opinion to counteract an APS made on behalf of the insured. IMEs may be conducted to help the insurer properly adjudicate the claim and find the cause, extent, and medical treatment of an illness or injury. The IME also aids the insurer to assess the impact of the potentially disabling illness as it relates to the insured's employment.

SOCIAL SECURITY DISABILITY INSURANCE

If an individual is out of work and receiving disability benefits from his or her disability income insurance, he or she can apply for Social Security disability benefits at any time. Generally, it takes about three to six months to get a decision on an application for **Social Security Disability Insurance (SSDI)**. If you get rejected you can appeal within 60 days of receiving a decision, but that

43

process can take many months. A small percentage of applicants for SSDI are approved on their first attempt without needing an appeal. If you receive SSDI benefits, after a 24-month qualifying period, you become eligible for Medicare. You may be also able to get Medicaid during this qualifying period. Once the individual receives SSDI, benefits under his or her disability income insurance policy cease.

BUSINESS OVERHEAD EXPENSE

Business overhead expense (BOE) insurance provides coverage for the owner should he or she become disabled. BOE is meant to cover the routine, normal overhead costs. Overhead expense coverage is not equivalent to personal disability insurance. A business overhead expense policy provides benefits for a shorter benefit period of about one to two years after a waiting period is completed. This coverage is useful in preventing the business from shutting down, being sold, or going into debt if the owner becomes disabled. These policies also work in circumstances where there is more than one owner. If the business is a partnership, each partner can obtain a BOE policy to provide protection for his or her individual share of the costs of running the business.

BUSINESS DISABILITY BUYOUT

A **disability buyout insurance policy** helps businesses succeed through difficult transitions. The policy allows either of the remaining owners—or the business entity itself—to purchase the disabled owner's share of the business at a previously agreed-upon price based on a formula that was put in place at the time the policy was issued. The owner who has become disabled is guaranteed a purchaser who is willing to pay the agreed-upon price for his or her share of the business. With this policy in place, there are no prolonged negotiations on the sale price. The benefit to the remaining owner(s) is that he or she (they) receive adequate funding through the insurance policy to buy the shares in the business rather than trying to seek an outside investor.

GROUP DISABILITY INCOME

Group disability income is a benefit providing disability insurance to employees either on a short-term basis, long-term basis, or both. Group disability is sponsored by the employer.

Short-term benefits are available for up to one or two years, but most frequently the short-term benefit period is set by the company at one year. Short-term policies typically use shorter elimination periods, such as 15 or 30 days.

Unlike individual disability income insurance, group coverage is not portable when an employee leaves for another job. Often, group policies do not use the own occupation definition of disability that covers enrollees more widely when they become disabled. Remember, own occupation disability policies will payout disability benefits if the insured can't perform his or her current job, regardless of his or her ability to work in any other position.

Under most group disability income policies, the premiums are paid for by the employer on a **tax-deductible basis**. The plans utilized by the employer may be funded through payroll deduction, and under most arrangements the employees pay all or part of the premiums for the coverage. In a **payroll deduction plan**, it is normal practice that any portions provided by the insured will not be tax-deductible to them. Payroll deduction plans may use individual disability income policies rather than group policies, especially when the entire premium is being paid by the employee.

Disability benefits received by the insured will be taxed as income.

KEY EMPLOYEE OR PARTNER DISABILITY

When a disability arises for a key employee, partner disability or key employee insurance policies help protect companies from the income loss. Small or medium-size business tend to benefit the most from these policies because they tend to rely heavily upon key employees more so than large corporations. These policies work by the business purchasing a disability insurance policy on a key employee, paying the premiums, and the business is the entity named as the beneficiary on the policy. Since it owns the policy, the business may surrender it, borrow against it, or use either the cash value or death benefits as the business chooses.

ACCIDENTAL DEATH AND DISMEMBERMENT (AD&D)

Accidental death and dismemberment (AD&D) insurance offers benefits when a serious accident occurs that results in an insured:

- Being seriously injured
- Losing a limb
- Losing an eye(s) or vision
- Being killed

The insured or beneficiary will only collect benefits from the policy if the death or injuries result directly from the accident.

Dismemberment coverage works on a per-member basis. Here's how insurers normally disburse benefits when an insured is hurt in an accident:

- Losing a hand, foot, limb, or sight in one eye usually results in 50 percent of the plan's full benefit
- Losing two limbs usually means 100 percent of the covered benefit
- Partial or complete paralysis generally means either 25 or 50 percent of the covered benefit

BASIC HOSPITAL (MEDICAL AND SURGICAL)

A **basic hospital plan** offers low-cost basic financial protection from large health care costs. This is a standalone policy that appeals to young and healthy individuals who do not require frequent medical services or could not otherwise qualify or afford major medical insurance. Also commonly referred to as a catastrophic plan, basic hospital insurance typically covers:

- Hospitalization and inpatient care
- Prescription drug coverage during inpatient treatment
- Surgery
- Other services performed on an outpatient basis (excluding prescription drugs)
- Emergency room services

The monthly premium is the cost of keeping health coverage through the carrier, and in return, health care expenses are subsidized by the plan carrier. There are usually, but not always, copayments required of the insured for health care used. **Copayments** are a fee typically paid by the insured at the time of service for the physician or health facility visit. They are generally a fraction of the total cost of a health care visit.

MAJOR MEDICAL INSURANCE

Generally **major medical insurance** policies provide coverage for inpatient, emergency care, and outpatient hospital services. Below are additional services that are typically covered under a major medical insurance plan:

- Physician services, including routine and basic visits for a specific illness or injury or preventive care at a clinic
- Prescription drug coverage
- Laboratory and diagnostic tests
- Durable medical equipment
- Physical therapy and chiropractic care
- Surgery
- Mental health treatment and counseling

Often these plans are offered as one of four different types: HMO, PPO, EPO, or POS.

HEALTH MAINTENANCE ORGANIZATION (HMO)

Providers contracted with a **health maintenance organization (HMO)** do not receive traditional payment as each health care service is rendered. Instead, HMO physicians receive a **capitated monthly rate** up front to provide health care to enrolled members. Because physicians contracted with the HMO are paid a set rate per month for each patient they see, they have built-in incentives to provide cost-efficient and effective care and avoid overutilization of services. Therefore, the HMO arrangement places risk upon the contracted providers within the HMO to effectively manage the care of enrollees within that capitated pay scale.

Under this arrangement, preventive care is paramount to avoid as many serious health conditions among the HMO population as possible. To help accomplish this, primary care providers also act as gatekeepers providing referrals to HMO-contracted specialists who provide non-preventive, specialized services. Most HMOs will not allow insureds see a specialist without these primary care provider referrals; however, some HMOs forego this gatekeeper element. HMOs rarely cover out-of-network providers, but they usually are the most affordable type of health insurance.

PREFERRED AND EXCLUSIVE PROVIDER ORGANIZATION

A **preferred provider organization (PPO)** is a group of contracted doctors, hospitals, pharmacies, and other health care providers who provide services at a negotiated discount to plan members. Negotiated discounts are typically 10-25% of the physician's usual, customary, and reasonable (UCR) charges that are billed to non-PPO member patients. Obtaining care from a PPO member provider means lower fees for policyholders; however, unlike HMOs, non-network doctors are still covered but without the PPO discount. You also do not need a referral to see a specialist. This increased flexibility means premiums are usually higher than HMOs. **Exclusive provider organizations (EPOs)** only cover services provided by medical professionals and facilities in the network, except in some cases of emergency.

POINT-OF-SERVICE PLAN

In a **point-of-service (POS)** plan, members select a primary physician in the network who can then refer them to specialists or services outside of the network, albeit at reduced coverage. The level of coverage depends on whether individuals choose health services from a plan provider, which is usually reimbursed at 90-100%, or from a non-plan provider, which is usually reimbursed in a fee-for-service arrangement at around 70 percent. The insured is responsible for any charges not paid by the insurer.

46

HEALTH SAVINGS ACCOUNTS, HEALTH REIMBURSEMENT ARRANGEMENTS, AND FLEXIBLE SPENDING ACCOUNTS

A flexible spending account (**FSA**), health savings account (**HSA**), and health reimbursement arrangement (**HRA**) all help pay medical expenses and are funded, at least in part, with pre-tax dollars. They are all different in the kind of insurance plan they work with, who has ownership of them, and who funds them.

An **HSA** is a tax advantaged savings/checking account designed for use with a high-deductible health plan (HDHP). Funds in the account are owned by the insured, but the account can be opened by either the individual or by an employer. An HSA is typically funded by pre-tax payroll deductions, but anyone can contribute funds to an HSA up to the federal limit each year. In order for these contributions to be tax-free, the insured must be covered by an HDHP. If the insured loses health coverage or switches to a plan that is not an HDHP, he or she retains the funds in the HSA, but may not continue to make tax-free contributions to it. Because there is no deadline to allocate or spend the funds in the HSA, account owners may accrue interest or even invest the funds in many cases. Funds in an HSA can only be withdrawn to pay for qualified medical expenses. Funds withdrawn for any other purpose are subject to both taxation and a 20% IRS penalty.

An **HRA** is a policy established by an employer to reimburse covered employees for qualified medical expenses that they incur. This means that unlike an HSA, an HRA is not something that stays with an individual through an employment change or retirement. It is also not an account; it has no enduring cash value to the insured. It is fully funded by the employer, which also makes all administrative decisions (within the boundaries of established federal guidelines), such as what types of expenses are covered, how much to reimburse, how the reimbursement process works, and whether unused HRA funds will roll over to the next year. Employees are not taxes on funds they receive through an HRA as it is considered a reimbursement as opposed to income.

An **FSA** is only available with employer-based health plans and is set up by the employer, so like an HRA, an FSA does not persist through an employment change or retirement. It is funded by tax-free payroll deductions, and the employer can also contribute. The money in the account does not roll over each year indefinitely like an HSA, so any funds not used by the end of the year disappear. There are two allowable **exceptions** to this rule that employers can offer. The first is that the employer can establish a grace period of up to two and a half months after the calendar year ends for employees to use their funds. The second is that the employer can allow employees to rollover up to $550 into the next year. Employers may offer only one of these two options.

In addition to more obvious qualified expenses like physician office visits and prescription drugs, HSA, HRA, and FSA funds can be used to pay for things such as:

- Blood glucose monitors and test strips
- Blood pressure monitors
- Hearing aid batteries
- First aid kits
- Eye glass accessories or contact solution
- Denture cream

Qualified medical expenses are defined by the IRS and include costs that relate to disease deterrence, diagnosis, and treatment. Expenses for cosmetic purposes, such as liposuction and Botox treatments, are generally not qualified. Some expenses like personal trainers are only qualified if they are prescribed by a doctor for specific medical reasons.

HIGH-DEDUCTIBLE HEALTH PLAN (HDHP)

HSAs have been growing steadily in popularity since their introduction in 2003 as part of the **Medicare Prescription Drug, Improvement, and Modernization Act**. To have an HSA you need a **high-deductible health plan (HDHP)**. The HDHP is like a traditional health plan, but it has uniquely high deductibles and lower premiums. It still covers routine preventive services, so it could be beneficial for someone who doesn't need to use many other services. This gives the insured a higher financial stake and financial incentive in health care decisions. By federal law, individuals can only open an HSA if they are enrolled in an HDHP and are not enrolled in other forms of low-deductible health insurance.

A high deductible health plan (HDHP) is a health insurance plan that meets federal guidelines in two benefit areas:

- Deductible
- Out-of-pocket maximum

These amounts are adjusted each calendar year by the IRS. For example, for 2022, an HDHP is any plan with a deductible of at least $1,400 for one person and $2,800 for a family. The out-of-pocket maximum can't be higher than $7,050 for one person and $14,100 for a family.

STOP-LOSS INSURANCE

Stop-loss insurance is coverage for businesses that self-fund, or self-insure, their own employee health benefit plans. These companies decide to cover the health care expenses for their employees with their own funds rather than pay premiums to an insurance company to cover expenses. Stop-loss insurance gives employers an extra level of protection in case the total health insurance claims of employees exceed the company's defined threshold. To accomplish the administration of coverage, these businesses contract with a third party to administer the health plan and handle processing claims.

There are two types of stop-loss insurance—specific and aggregate:

- **Specific stop-loss insurance** provides coverage when the claims of any individual employee exceed a preset level defined in the policy. This is meant to prevent any extreme losses that might be incurred due to the medical expenses of a single employee.
- **Aggregate stop-loss insurance** provides coverage when the total claims of the whole group (not a single individual) eclipse a preset level defined in the policy, such as 125 percent of the projected cost of claims.

BECOMING ELIGIBLE FOR MEDICARE BENEFITS

There are three different ways someone can become eligible for Medicare. First, when individuals reach 65, they become eligible to enroll in both Medicare Parts A and B. Second, if individuals receive either Social Security Disability Insurance (SSDI) or Railroad Retirement Board (RRB) disability benefits, they become eligible for Medicare after 24 months. A third way to become eligible for Medicare is to have one of two specific diagnoses. If an individual is not yet 65 but has been diagnosed with either end-stage renal disease (ESRD) or amyotrophic lateral sclerosis (ALS), commonly known as Lou Gehrig's disease, he or she becomes eligible for Medicare. Once an individual is diagnosed with ALS, it is important he or she immediately applies for SSDI to be eligible for Medicare. Once approved, the insured will automatically be enrolled in Medicare the first month he or she receives benefits. There is no waiting period for Medicare for those diagnosed with ALS or ESRD.

MEDICARE SUPPLEMENT POLICIES

Sold by private companies, **Medicare supplement plans**, also known as **Medigap,** can help pay some of the health care costs that Original Medicare doesn't cover, such as copayments, coinsurance, and deductibles or medical care when you travel outside the US. If you have Original Medicare and a Medigap policy, the former will pay its share of the Medicare-approved amount for covered health care costs and then the Medigap policy pays its share.

Medicare pays for many preventive services to help enrollees stay healthy. For individuals enrolled in Original Medicare, they will often not have any coinsurance or deductible requirements for specific preventive care services if they see a physician or other health care provider who accepts assignment. Doctors who accept assignment cannot charge an individual more than the Medicare-approved amount. There are many different preventive services that are covered, including:

- Exams
- Shots
- Lab tests and health screenings
- Yearly wellness visit programs for health monitoring
- Counseling and education

MEDICARE ADVANTAGE PLANS

A **Medicare Advantage (MA)** plan is different than a Medicare supplement plan. These plans are offered by private companies and provide Original Medicare and usually prescription drug coverage (Part D) and extra benefits not normally provided by Original Medicare. These plans include health maintenance organizations, preferred provider organizations, private fee-for-service plans, and special needs plans.

The Medicare program pays a fixed amount each month to the companies that are contracted to offer Medicare Advantage Plans and sets the rules for these companies to follow.

MEDICARE PART D PRESCRIPTION DRUG COVERAGE

Medicare Part D prescription drug coverage was created by the **Medicare Prescription Drug, Improvement, and Modernization Act of 2003**. Individuals who have Medicare Part A, Part B, or Medicare Advantage are eligible for prescription drug coverage under Part D. Joining a Medicare prescription drug plan is voluntary, and an additional monthly premium is required for the coverage. Some Medicare Advantage plans provide prescription coverage without an additional premium. Medicare beneficiaries are eligible to:

- Remain in the Original Medicare program without participating in Medicare Part D
- Remain in the Original Medicare program and enroll in a stand-alone Part D drug plan
- Enroll in a private Medicare Advantage plan that offers both Original Medicare and prescription drug coverage

Part D has four phases of coverage. The first is the deductible phase in which you pay the full cost of your prescriptions until you reach the deductible. The deductible varies among plans, but no plan may have one higher than $480 in 2022. Next is the initial coverage period in which you pay either a copay or coinsurance amount on each drug up until the limit of $4,430 in 2022. When you cross this threshold, you have entered the coverage gap, and you must pay 25 percent of the cost of each drug. You could pay more in the coverage gap phase if 25 percent of the drugs is higher than the coinsurance or copayment amount you paid in the initial coverage period. The fourth phase is the catastrophic coverage phase that you reach when your out-of-pocket costs exceed $7,050 in 2022. In this phase, your copay or coinsurance costs are very low (about 5 percent).

The coverage gap, sometimes referred to as the "donut hole," costs used to be higher than 25 percent and enrollees were responsible for 100 percent of drug costs in this phase, but the ACA helped enrollees by lowering that amount each year until it reached 25 percent in 2020.

ACA Changes

Within the federal **ACA rules**, Medicare coverage of certain preventive services is improved, including, among many other services and screenings, coverage for preventive mammograms, preventative colonoscopies, and yearly wellness visits. These types of preventative services are now covered without enrollees paying anything towards their Part B coinsurance or deductible. Diagnostic tests that are performed for the purpose of evaluating suspected illness or disease are not covered at 100 percent under the ACA since they are not preventive in nature.

Group vs. Individual Health Insurance Coverage

Most individuals who have health insurance through **group health coverage** access it as an employee through their employer. Others access group coverage due to their membership in an association such as a local union or industry trade association. **Individual health insurance** is coverage that a private individual acquires on his or her own without an employer's contribution or assistance from an affiliated organization. Depending on how many employees there are, benefits covered by a group plan versus individual plan can vary quite a bit. Plans sold in compliance with the ACA cover the same **10 essential health benefits**. These essential benefits include:

- Ambulatory services
- Chronic disease management, wellness care, and preventive services
- Emergency services
- Hospitalization
- Laboratory services
- Maternity and newborn care
- Mental health and substance abuse treatment
- Pediatric services, including dental and vision care
- Prescription drugs
- Rehabilitative and habilitative services

The 10 essential benefits are required as part of any ACA-compliant health plan, whether it is sold inside or outside the health insurance marketplace. This includes ACA-compliant plans for individual coverage and business coverage for businesses with fewer than 50 full-time employees.

Group Health Insurance Coverage

Group health insurance coverage is a policy that is purchased by an employer and is then offered to eligible employees (and most often their families) as an employee benefit. A group health insurance plan is a key component of many employee benefits packages that employers provide for their employees. Most Americans have group health insurance coverage through their employer or the employer of a family member. Some employers allow employees to choose between several different plans, including both indemnity insurance and managed care. Other employers offer only one plan.

These are two positive reasons for employees to select employer-sponsored group health insurance:

- One of the advantages for employees in a group health plan is the contribution most employers make toward the cost of the health coverage premium. In fact, most employers cover the largest portion of the health insurance premium.
- Another benefit is that in being covered by a group plan, the benefits are often more comprehensive and affordable than what would be available to the individual if he or she bought his or her own plan.

Employer-sponsored plans began expanding during World War II because of wage controls imposed on employers by the federal government. The labor market was difficult for employers because of the increased demand for goods and decreased supply of workers while America was at war. The wage and price controls imposed on employers did not allow them to increase wages sufficiently to attract employees. By offering health insurance to prospective employees, employers were able to recruit employees despite not being able to increase their wages. This change was able to occur, because the National War Labor Board ruled that **fringe benefits**, including sick leave and health insurance, did not apply as wages for the purpose of wage controls. As a result, employers began offering improved fringe benefit packages, including health care coverage.

Another means to access group coverage is through membership in a union, professional association, or other group. However, there must be a reason for the group's existence beyond the association's effort to obtain health insurance. An example might be individual realtors who form an association of realtors for professional purposes. Then later, they decide to use their association membership to apply to an insurer and obtain a group health insurance plan.

GROUP CONVERSION

Group health insurance plans must offer enrollees a **conversion plan** so enrollees have an option to continue coverage when group coverage is lost through their employer. However, a conversion plan is not a continuation of the enrollee's original group coverage. Instead, enrollees purchase a health care plan on their own through the insurance carrier that provided their group coverage. To continue coverage this way, the enrollee needs to complete an insurance application and pay the first month's premium to the insurer within 31 days of the end of the original group coverage or when the notice of coverage ending was received by the enrollee. The new plan will take effect without a lapse of coverage after the group coverage ends.

FEE-FOR-SERVICE PLANS

Fee-for-service plans, also called **indemnity plans**, are arrangements in which doctors and other health care providers are reimbursed for each individual service they render to insured patients, such as an office visit, laboratory test, or surgical procedure. The **allowable amount** is the amount that the insurer will pay for each given service, usually based on a negotiated fee schedule that is established with a group of health care providers. Under a fee-for-service plan, the insured is usually required to pay for services upfront and then seek reimbursement from the insurance company. As with other insurance policies, fee-for-service plans require insureds to pay a monthly premium, a deductible, and coinsurance.

STATE REGULATORY READABILITY STANDARDS

As health insurance benefits and coverage have become increasingly complex, state insurance regulators have attempted to create **readability standards.** Lawmakers implement these standards to make it easier for the public to understand health insurance documents. To accomplish this, insurance regulators have developed readability mechanisms to assess how readable an insurance policy document is or isn't. The more readable a document is, the more understandable it is to the average health insurance consumer.

- Most states require that a readability test of insurance documents score above some minimum value on the Flesch reading ease test—typically 40 or above.
- Many states have attempted to improve the readability of insurance forms to a tenth or eighth grade reading level to increase understanding of insurance policy language.

INSURANCE LICENSING AND CONTINUING EDUCATION

State regulators make sure health insurance agents and brokers are treating citizens fairly and professionally when it comes to their health insurance coverage. For example, state regulators mandate that individuals must pass a state insurance exam to gain a license for selling insurance coverage. In addition, states require that insurance agents routinely meet continuing education requirements to maintain their insurance licenses. To accomplish this, many states require agents to complete 24 hours of insurance education every two years.

DEFINED CONTRIBUTION HEALTH PLAN

Traditional group health insurance is provided on a **defined benefit basis** when an employer pays the costs to provide a specific group health plan benefit through an insurer. In contrast, some employers choose to provide a **defined contribution health plan**, which helps the employer to fix their health insurance benefit costs on a monthly basis.

When using a defined contribution health plan, employers give employees a specific dollar amount (a defined contribution) to apply to their benefit costs. Through these coverage plans, the employee, not the employer, manages the allocation of the money provided to meet his or her unique health care needs. The funds provided by the employer by the defined contribution health plan are used by employees to pay for the individual health insurance costs they incur.

Compared to traditional group health insurance coverage, these plans can be an affordable alternative for employers. Because these plans do not directly pay for health care provided by medical doctors, hospitals, and the like, they are not considered health insurance plans in the traditional sense.

OBTAINING HEALTH INSURANCE THROUGH AN ASSOCIATION

Many individuals gain access to group health insurance coverage through membership in a union, professional association, or other non-employer group. However, there must be a reason for the group's existence beyond the association's effort to obtain health insurance. For instance, individual dentists who form an association of dentists for professional and educational purposes can then use their association membership to get a group insurance plan, if they have no other access to affordable group health coverage. Forty-six states have approved associations to provide group health insurance coverage. The coverage must meet the laws of the states in which the coverage is offered.

VOLUNTARY BENEFITS PROGRAMS

Voluntary benefits programs have increasingly become a way in which employers offer health insurance programs and supplemental coverage for their employees. This type of coverage, while offered through an employer, is entirely paid for by the employee; however, by enrolling through their employer he or she pays reduced rates. For example, a **voluntary benefit** may pay an employee a lump sum if a policyholder becomes diagnosed with a serious medical condition.

Insureds can use the money to cover out-of-pocket medical costs they incur. There are a variety of voluntary benefits programs available to employees, including coverage for things like specific diseases (e.g., cancer), accidents, and hospitalizations.

COVERAGE FOR EMERGENCY CARE OUTSIDE THE UNITED STATES

One of the limitations of many medical insurance programs, including Medicare, is that they do not cover medical emergencies that occur outside the United States. That means a person who gets sick while on vacation abroad may have to personally pay for all the medical treatment costs. Even when individuals drive or walk across the US border to Mexico or Canada, they are most likely not covered by their existing health insurance plan. **Travel insurance** is designed to fill this gap and provide temporary coverage and reimbursement to individuals who incur health care costs while traveling abroad. With Medicare, enrollees may be able to add a **foreign travel benefit rider** with some Medigap plans to provide some coverage when abroad.

MANAGED CARE PLANS

Managed care is a method of health care delivery that seeks to control the costs of health care services and improve care quality through **precertification and utilization review**, which means the insurance company reviews proposed large dollar health care services to ensure appropriate and efficient care is rendered. **Managed care plans** contract with a group of selected providers and do not allow unfiltered access to all providers to their enrollees. To encourage the use of contracted providers, the managed care plan provides fewer benefits and less coverage when enrollees use noncontracted providers. Managed care organizations include health maintenance organizations (HMOs), preferred provider organizations (PPOs), and point-of-service (POS) plans.

COBRA

The federal **Consolidated Omnibus Budget Reconciliation Act of 1985 (COBRA)** added health care continuation requirements allowing individuals to keep their health insurance coverage for up to 18 months or longer under certain circumstances. When an individual leaves an employer, under certain circumstances, he or she can choose COBRA continuation to continue the same health coverage. COBRA continuation coverage permits employees and their dependents under a group health plan to continue their coverage if a **qualifying event** causes them to lose coverage. Among the qualifying events listed in the statute are:

- Voluntary or forced termination or reduced work hours
- Death of the insured
- Legal separation or divorce that ends an ex-spouse's coverage eligibility
- Loss of dependent child status

There are two circumstances under which an extension of COBRA continuation for up to an additional 18 months (beyond the original 18 months) may become available. This could occur either when the insured confronts a second qualifying event or when a qualified beneficiary is found to be disabled by the Social Security Administration. A second qualifying event could include:

- The death of the covered employee
- The divorce or legal separation of the covered employee and spouse
- The covered employee becoming entitled to Medicare

To get the extension, the qualified beneficiary must notify the plan administrator of an SSA disability determination or of the second qualifying event.

The **90-day COBRA continuation option** applies to employees of insured groups who become ineligible for coverage under the group policy. The continuation option also may be available to persons who lose coverage due to termination of the master group policy, unless the employee is eligible under a replacement group policy.

If an employee should lose eligibility for the group's coverage, he or she can continue group coverage for a period of 90 days under these circumstances:

- The person must have been enrolled for at least three months.
- The person must apply for coverage with the group administrator and prepay the total premium for the 90-day period prior to his or her termination.

HEALTH INSURANCE PORTABILITY AND ACCOUNTABILITY ACT (HIPAA)

HIPAA requires covered entities and business associates to comply with certain security and privacy requirements to protect the confidentiality of **protected health information (PHI)**. **Covered entity** means:

- A health plan
- A health care clearinghouse
- A health care provider who transmits any health information electronically related to transactions regulated by HIPAA

A **health plan** means individual or group coverage that provides or pays for health care services (e.g., health insurance companies, Medicare, Medicaid, etc.). An employer is not typically a covered entity as defined under the HIPAA law.

A **health care clearinghouse** is an entity that processes health care information.

Health care providers include doctors, dentists, and nursing homes, among many others.

Business associates are people or companies who provide services for covered entities, such as data analysis or claims processing.

A **small employer group** for health insurance purposes was defined by HIPAA as consisting of 2-50 employees. Federal law requires all plans sold to small groups to be a **guaranteed issue** health insurance plan. This means small employers cannot be denied coverage by an insurer based on the health of their employees.

HIPAA provided **creditable coverage guarantees** so that a person could not be subject due to a preexisting condition exclusion if he or she were leaving a job for a new one with less than a 63-day gap in health insurance coverage. With the passage of the ACA and its elimination of the ability for insurance companies to deny coverage for preexisting conditions, many of these provisions were rendered obsolete.

AFFORDABLE CARE ACT (ACA)

The language of the ACA originally required individuals without health insurance benefits through their employers to purchase coverage or pay a tax penalty. However, the passage of the Tax Cuts and Jobs Act in 2017 eliminated this penalty, effectively nullifying the individual mandate. Lower income persons receive subsidies to purchase coverage through the health insurance marketplace.

Key ACA provisions include:

- Insurers may not cancel insurance coverage when insureds become ill.
- Federal and state health insurance marketplaces (or exchanges) were created, giving businesses and individuals the ability to compare plans and enroll in coverage in one place.
- Children can remain on their parents' health insurance plans until they turn 26, regardless of dependent status or marital status.
- Insurers are required to cover many types of preventive care, such as immunizations and screening for common diseases, at no expense to the insured.
- Insurers may no longer place lifetime or annual limits on an insured's covered medical care.
- Insurers may not deny coverage to individuals because of preexisting conditions (including pregnancy).
- Insurers must offer the same premiums for insureds within the same age and geographical groups without discrimination based on gender or preexisting conditions. Insurers are still allowed to rate tobacco users at a higher rate than non-tobacco users.

LONG-TERM CARE INSURANCE

Long-term care insurance covers a range of services and supports individuals to meet their personal care needs and maintain their independence. Most long-term care is not medical care, but rather assistance with the basic personal tasks of everyday living, called **activities of daily living (ADLs)**. ADLs are activities like bathing, dressing, and eating. A **long-term care (LTC) insurance policy** helps cover the expenses of extended care for people who need help with these activities. The services covered by LTC insurance are not covered by private group or individual health insurance plans or Medicare. Medicaid, however, does provide some long-term care but not nearly as comprehensively as LTC insurance. Long-term care insurance covers the expenses incurred for **skilled or unskilled care** provided in:

- Nursing homes
- Assisted living facilities
- Adult day care services
- Hospice care
- In-home care (this may include homemaker services like grocery shopping or housekeeping)
- Home adaptations
- Care management services

HOME HEALTH CARE

With advancements in medical technologies, people are living increasingly longer lives and therefore, staying in their homes longer. Long-term care insurance provides coverage for activities of daily living (ADLs) such as bathing, eating, and dressing. Individuals with chronic diseases often have trouble performing some of these ADLs, and the need for assistance with these activities is how an individual becomes eligible for long-term care insurance benefits. More and more elderly

Americans are using home health care in their homes through long-term care insurance policies to stay independent and in their homes longer, rather than transitioning to a nursing home.

ACTIVITIES OF DAILY LIVING

The most common ADLs used for determining benefits in a long-term care insurance policy are:

- Bathing
- Continence
- Dressing
- Eating
- Toileting (moving on and off the toilet)
- Transferring (getting in and out of bed)

These functions are considered essential in everyday, healthy, and functional living without major assistance from friends, family, and caregivers. If an individual needs assistance in performing two or three of these (depending on the long-term care insurance contract language) then that person may be eligible for long-term care benefits.

DAILY BENEFIT

Long-term care insurance coverage for nursing home care is based on a **daily benefit** stipulated in the policy. The benefit amount usually is a daily benefit ranging from $50 to $300 or more per day. An insured may choose a benefit period that is a specific number of days, months, or years. A **maximum benefit period** may range from one year to the remainder of the insured's lifetime.

ELIMINATION PERIOD

Under a long-term care insurance policy, the **elimination period** is the number of days between when the insured starts needing care and when the insured starts receiving payments for the care services. During this time, the insured must pay for his or her care out of pocket. The **schedule of benefits page** in a long-term care insurance policy states the specific elimination period of the insured's policy.

During the elimination period the insured must become chronically ill and receive primary services (other than hospice care and respite care) before certain benefits become payable. Benefits will not be paid for covered services the policyholder receives during this time. No elimination period is required for the insured to receive benefits for hospice care, respite care, needs assessment or informal caregiver training. The days that count toward the elimination period might or might not be required to be consecutive days. The need to not be consecutive days is helpful to the insured if his or her initial home care treatment does not take place every day.

The elimination period, under most policies, needs to be met just once.

WAIVER OF PREMIUM RIDER

A popular rider that insureds often attach to their long-term care insurance policy is the **waiver of premium rider**. With this waiver the insured can benefit from an insurance policy even when he or she is unable to work or to pay for coverage. In other words, the insured isn't required to pay premiums while receiving benefits. To use the waiver, the policyholder needs to be disabled for a specified amount of time, such as three months or six months.

For an added fee, most insurance companies will incorporate this waiver into the policy. The waiver is usually associated with life insurance and long-term care policies and usually isn't available with health or disability income policies.

INFLATION RIDER

As long-term care costs continue to rise much faster than the rate of inflation, insurers have an important rider for consumers to consider purchasing to add value to their policy over the long haul. Many states now require it as an option in insurer's LTC insurance policies. Some insurers include it as part the policy itself while others offer it as an **inflation protection rider**.

Plans that include automatic inflation increases use two different methods—either a simple or a compound method—to increase the coverage of a daily benefit by a set percentage.

- Typically, insurers use a **simple method** in which the original daily benefit increases by the same percentage each year, typically 3-5%. That means a $200 daily benefit with a simple rider of 5 percent would increase by $10.00 every year.
- The **compound method** means the increase is by the percentage of the previous year's total daily benefit, not the original daily benefit. For example, if the compound rider is 5 percent and the original daily benefit is $200, then in the first year it would go up to $210. In the second year, it would go up by 5 percent of $210, so it would go up to $220.50. In the third year, it would go up by 5 percent of $220.50, and so on.

COUPLING LONG-TERM CARE INSURANCE WITH A LIFE INSURANCE POLICY

The life insurance and long-term care insurance combination product provides a unique benefit package leveraging both life and long-term care insurance. Some individuals consider it a waste to pay long-term care insurance premiums and possibly never need long-term care. The provisions of the **Pension Protection Act (PPA) of 2006** provide tax benefits for these long-term care combination plans. These new benefits apply for annuity contracts and life insurance policies. The PPA permits the tax-free distribution of a life insurance or annuity cash value to pay for long-term care. These plans work by tapping the life insurance policy's death benefit and using it to pay for long-term care if needed. The benefit is drawn down to pay for care and whatever is used reduces the total balance of the life insurance benefit.

FACILITIES WHERE CARE IS A COVERED BENEFIT

Most long-term care is provided at home by health care attendants or nurses. Other kinds of long-term care services and supports are provided by community service organizations and in long-term care facilities such as assisted living centers, nursing homes, and continuing care retirement communities. An example of home care services includes nursing care and/or therapy provided by nurses or therapists who come to the home on a routine schedule. Examples of community support services include transportation services and adult day care services. Home care agencies often provide daily services or on an as-needed basis.

COVERAGE LIMITATION RELATED TO THE THREE-DAY HOSPITAL STAY FOR SKILLED NURSING CARE

Medicare provides coverage for a **skilled nursing facility (SNF)** when enrollees have an inpatient hospital stay of at least three consecutive days and the individual enters the SNF within 30 days of that inpatient hospital stay.

- Medicare coverage is up to 20 days in an SNF for each benefit period without the patient being responsible for any portion of the costs.
- The Medicare enrollee is responsible for coinsurance costs for days 21-100 in each benefit period.
- The Medicare enrollee is responsible for all SNF care costs from day 101 and beyond.

57

INTERACTION OF A LONG-TERM CARE PARTNERSHIP PROGRAM WITH STATE MEDICAID INSURANCE

An alternative to traditional long-term care insurance is a qualified state **long-term care partnership program**. Partnership programs are an innovative cooperative between private insurance carriers and state governments to address the financing of long-term care and reduce pressure on state Medicaid programs. In states with LTC partnership programs in place, the state's Medicaid program eligibility requirements are adjusted so that potential insureds have financial incentives to buy private LTC coverage. The partnership plans work by allowing those with long-term care insurance benefits that have been exhausted under an insurance policy to apply and get benefits through Medicaid. So, if the cost of his or her care exceeds the insurance policy's benefit level, the insured can apply for and receive additional long-term care coverage under Medicaid, thus creating a partnership.

CRITICAL ILLNESS POLICIES VS. TRADITIONAL HEALTH INSURANCE COVERAGE

Traditional health insurance reimburses the provider for covered medical services, procedures, equipment, etc. A critical illness plan, in contrast, pays the insured person directly if he or she is diagnosed with a covered critical illness. When there is a claim, modern critical illness policies usually provide a lump-sum benefit to the insured. Benefit payments can be used to cover things such as:

- Medical expenses
- Lost wages at work for insured and family
- Child-care expenses
- Travel expenses for insured and family

VERIFYING BENEFIT ELIGIBILITY UNDER CRITICAL ILLNESS COVERAGE PLANS

A critical illness diagnosis must be verified by the insurer prior to the policy providing any benefits. The insurer will require that the diagnosis needs to have been identified after the policy's effective date or else it is deemed a preexisting condition and coverage will be denied. To verify a cancer diagnosis, most insurance companies require the receipt of a pathology report of a biopsy performed on the insured. If a biopsy cannot be performed due to medical reasons, a clinical diagnosis may be allowed by the insurer.

PAYING BENEFITS TO AN INSURED COVERED BY A CANCER OR CRITICAL ILLNESS PLAN

Critical illness policies typically cover medical emergencies like strokes, heart attacks, organ transplants, cancer, and other life-altering conditions. The purpose of critical illness plans is to help insureds offset the enormous costs of medical care and help replace lost wages after experiencing a medical emergency.

If an insured or insured dependent is diagnosed with a covered critical illness, the insurer will typically pay out a **lump-sum cash payment** to the insured to use in whatever ways he or she chooses. Unlike traditional health insurance, a hospital or physician does not submit claims to the insurer for coverage and reimbursement. The policy's proceeds can be used by the insured to cover payments toward his or her mortgage, medical bills, and living expenses while recuperating. The insured can also apply the benefit funds to experimental medical treatments not covered by his or her health insurance policy.

Cancer insurance is specific in providing coverage only when the patient has received a diagnosis of a covered cancer. Specified disease or cancer insurance policies offer coverage only to those conditions specifically identified within the policy. Ancillary treatments that are not related to the diagnosis may be denied as not eligible under the policy. This is typical of other disease plans as well.

GROUP HOSPITAL INDEMNITY COVERAGE

Group hospital indemnity coverage can help insureds manage an unexpected medical crisis. The coverage provides a lump-sum benefit when an insured is admitted to a hospital on an inpatient basis. The insured can then use that lump-sum benefit as he or she sees fit. The plan pays the fixed benefits based on the coverage level chosen by the insured.

These benefits may include services such as the following:

- Both inpatient and outpatient surgery
- Inpatient hospital stays for an accident or illness
- Inpatient physician visits and diagnostic testing
- Ambulance transport
- Emergency room treatment

DENTAL INSURANCE

Coverage for dental services provided within dental insurance plans is generally categorized into four distinct categories:

- **Preventive coverage** includes routine cleanings and exams to prevent dental issues and deterioration of teeth.
- **Basic services** generally include teeth cleanings, x-rays, and cavity fillings.
- **Major services** in dental coverage typically include more intensive restorative services such as crowns, root canals, and dental surgery to repair and restore damaged teeth.
- **Orthodontic** coverage includes braces and other appliances to realign or shift teeth to allow better spacing and alignment of teeth.

ACA DENTAL PLANS

Dental benefits under the ACA are not an essential benefit offered for adults within health insurance marketplace plans, but they are sometimes included. There are **stand-alone dental plans** available; however, for children under 18, the ACA defines dental treatment as an essential benefit.

There are two types of dental plan options available through the marketplace: **high and low dental coverage** plans. The details are as follows:

- The **high coverage level** has higher premiums but reduced copayments and deductibles.
- The **low coverage level** has lower premiums but higher copayments and deductibles.

VISION INSURANCE

Vision insurance is generally a supplemental policy sold along with a medical insurance plan. However, like dental care, vision care is an essential benefit for children. Vision insurance generally covers or provides a discount toward vision care and optical products. For example, vision coverage can help individuals reduce the costs they incur for routine eye exams, as well as vision correction wear that may be prescribed by an optometrist or ophthalmologist. This means items such as eyeglass frames, eyeglass lenses, and contact lenses are typically provided for within vision care insurance plans. Some vision care plans require that the insured see a provider in the plan's network.

Individual insureds typically sign up on their own vision plan rather than through an association or an employer. The individual then pays a monthly premium for the vision coverage. For vision insurance through an employer group plan, the premium is often deducted from the insured's paycheck.

Most medical insurance policies will cover vision claims as they relate to an injury or a medical condition (e.g., diabetes).

Types of Health Policies Chapter Quiz

1. When analyzing a claim under a disability income insurance policy, the insurer often seeks to verify the insured's statement regarding the illness or injury by:

   a. Confirming that the insured is out of work
   b. Requesting an attending physician's statement
   c. Engaging an insurance underwriter to investigate
   d. Soliciting a point-of-service payments record

2. Which of the following provides coverage for the owner of a business should he or she become disabled, and is meant to cover normal operating expenses?

   a. Social Security disability insurance
   b. Key employee or partner insurance
   c. Business overhead expense insurance
   d. Disability buyout insurance

3. Which of the following is commonly referred to as a "catastrophic plan"?

   a. Basic hospital plan
   b. Medigap
   c. Payroll deduction plan
   d. Accidental death and dismemberment

4. Providers contracted with which of the following do not receive traditional payment, but instead the physicians receive a capitated monthly rate up front to provide health care to the enrolled members?

   a. Health maintenance organization (HMO)
   b. Preferred provider organization (PPO)
   c. Exclusive provider organization (EPO)
   d. Point of service (POS) plan

5. What do an FSA, HSA, and HRA all have in common?

   a. They are all owned by the insured
   b. They are all funded by payroll deductions
   c. They all work with the same kind of insurance plans
   d. They are all at least partially funded with pre-tax dollars

6. When were health savings accounts (HSA) introduced?

   a. 2000
   b. 2001
   c. 2002
   d. 2003

7. Which of the following is NOT one of the different ways someone can become eligible for Medicare?

   a. Reach the age of 65
   b. Receive either Social Security Disability Insurance (SSDI) or Railroad Retirement Board (RRB) disability benefits for 24 months
   c. Experience a serious accident resulting in either serious injury, including loss of a limb, eye, or eyesight, or partial or complete paralysis
   d. Diagnosed with either end-stage renal disease or amyotrophic lateral sclerosis

8. What phase of Part D Medicare is sometimes referred to as the "donut hole"?

a. Initial coverage phase
b. Coverage gap phase
c. Deductible phase
d. Catastrophic coverage phase

9. Why did employer-sponsored health plans begin to expand during World War II?

a. Because providers wanted to avoid group conversion
b. Because unions and professional associations were dominating the labor market
c. Because of an increased supply of uneducated workers
d. Because of wage controls imposed on employers by the federal government

10. Fee-for-service plans are also called:

a. Indemnity plans
b. Conversion plans
c. Advantage plans
d. Supplement plans

11. Because it does not directly pay for health care, which of the following is not considered a health insurance plan in the traditional sense?

a. Voluntary benefit plans
b. Defined contribution health plans
c. Indemnity insurance plans
d. Defined benefit health plans

12. Which of the following is NOT a circumstance under which an extension of COBRA continuation for up to an additional 18 months (beyond the original 18 months) may become available?

a. The qualified beneficiary is found to be disabled by the SSA
b. The divorce or legal separation of the covered employee and spouse
c. The covered employee becoming entitled to Medicare
d. The loss of replacement group policy eligibility

13.Which of the following is not typically a covered entity as defined under the HIPAA law?

a. A health care clearinghouse
b. A health plan
c. An employer
d. A health care provider

14. Which of the following is typically not medical care, but rather assistance with the basic personal tasks of everyday living?

a. Long-term care
b. Affordable care
c. Managed care
d. Emergency care

15. Under a long-term care insurance policy, the number of days between when the insured starts needing care and when the insured starts receiving payments for the care services is referred to as the:
   a. Daily benefit payout
   b. Elimination period
   c. Schedule of benefits
   d. Primary service phase

16. Which of the following do many states now require as an option in insurer's long-term care (LTC) insurance policies?
   a. Foreign benefit rider
   b. Waiver of premium rider
   c. Inflation protection rider
   d. Return-of-premium rider

17. The provisions of the Pension Protection Act (PPA) of 2006 provide tax benefits for:
   a. The simple method for automatic inflation increases
   b. Accidental death and dismemberment plans
   c. LTC and life insurance combination plans
   d. Health insurance through an association

18. Which of the following works by allowing those with LTC insurance benefits that have been exhausted under an insurance policy to apply and get benefits through Medicaid?
   a. Voluntary benefits programs
   b. Anti-money laundering programs
   c. Wellness programs
   d. Long-term care partnership programs

19. With what policy can the proceeds be used by the insured in whatever way he or she chooses e.g., to cover mortgage payments, medical bills, or living expenses?
   a. Critical illness policies
   b. Major medical insurance policies
   c. Traditional health policies
   d. Business overhead expense policies

20. What category of coverage provided within dental insurance plans generally includes teeth cleanings, x-rays, and cavity fillings?
   a. Preventive coverage
   b. Basic services
   c. Major services
   d. Orthodontic coverage

Health Policy Revisions, Clauses, and Riders

ENTIRE CONTRACT CLAUSE

The entire contract clause states that all pieces of the agreement between insurer and insured are found in the contract. This clause functions primarily for the protection of the insured. It means that the insurance policy along with the application and any added conditions represent the entire contract sold to the insured. After the insurance policy documents are issued, the insurer is allowed zero discretion thereafter in making changes to the contract or policy. Once a policy has been issued, the only changes permitted are those proposed and made by the policyholder themselves through endorsements, riders, or amendments. This clause, therefore, keeps the insurance company from making arbitrary changes to the policy provisions when the insured files a claim.

INCONTESTABILITY CLAUSE

The incontestability clause prohibits an insurer from voiding coverage after a defined period of time because of an insured's misstatement on the insurance application. Typically, an incontestability clause stipulates that after two or three years, a policy cannot be voided or terminated due to a misstatement of fact by the policyholder. Incontestability provisions are mandated by state insurance regulators to provide protection for insureds against insurance carriers who may try to evade claims payments. While this provision benefits the insured, it must be noted that it does not protect against outright fraud or lies within an insurance application. A policyholder's intention to deceive an insurer can cause the coverage to be cancelled or possibly result in the filing of criminal fraud charges.

RIDERS

A rider is an amendment to an insurance policy. Riders to health insurance plans typically add coverage for a slightly higher premium. An exclusionary rider was an amendment that used to be allowed in individual health insurance policies that permanently excluded coverage for a health condition, body part, or body system. With the enactment of the ACA, starting in September 2010, exclusionary riders became prohibited and no longer were able to be applied to coverage for children. Starting in 2014, exclusionary riders became prohibited on any health insurance coverage.

GRACE PERIOD

A **grace period** is a policy provision that grants the insured generally either 30 or 31 days after the effective date to make his or her payment without the risk of the coverage lapsing. If the payment is not made by the end of the grace period, then the coverage terminates retroactively to the end date of the previous premium payment.

Under the ACA, if a patient who receives an advance premium tax credit does not pay his or her health insurance premiums in full, he or she enters a grace period of 90 days. During the first 30 days of the grace period, the insured will continue to have health insurance coverage, and the health insurer will pay claims. However, if the insured enters the grace period's second or third month, the insurer may pend claims for care during this time. If the insured provides the full premium payment by the grace period's end, the insured retains his or her coverage, and the insurer is required to pay the pended claims. If the premium is not paid, the coverage will end after the first month and claims occurring thereafter will be denied.

Policy Reinstatement

If premiums are not paid within the grace period, insurers may choose to reinstate the policy without requiring an application. However, the insurer may require an application to decide on the reinstatement of the policy. If the policy is reinstated, the insurer will honor claims that occurred after the reinstatement date. Both the insured and the insurance carrier will retain the rights that existed before the policy ended, subject to any conditions attached to the new policy upon reinstatement.

Notice of Claim Provision

One required standard inclusion in insurance policies is the **notice of claim provision**, as it is required by state law. The notice of claim provision mandates that the insured provide information to the insurance company concerning a covered loss under the policy as soon as possible. Late notice of a covered loss may hamper the ability of the insurance company to complete its review and accurately determine whether the insured is eligible for benefits. Failure by the insured to act in a timely manner to provide notice of a claim could result in the insurance company not being required to make the claims payments.

Proof of Loss Provision

The **proof of loss provision** requires the insured to submit insurance claims to the insurer in a timely manner. The requirement of timeliness is in place to mandate that the insurance company fulfill its obligations promptly but also to allow it to fully investigate the claim as thoroughly as it needs and without unnecessary delay. This provision places the burden on the insurer to act in an appropriate and speedy manner, not the insured, as insurance companies are responsible for paying claims as soon as they have adequate proof of loss. This provision put a greater burden on the insurer to provide clear, direct, and fair payment of insurance claims.

Processing of Claims Related to Disability Income Insurance

To receive benefits under a disability income insurance plan, the insured is required to file a claim with the insurer in a timely manner. The insured will also likely be required to submit an attending physician's statement (APS) to aid in proving the existence of a covered disability. This statement is perhaps the most important element in the claims process. The insurance company or the employer will then review the claim and the APS. The submitted information will help the insurer conclude as to whether the individual should receive disability benefits under the policy.

CMS-1500 Claims Forms

The **CMS-1500 form** is the official Medicare and Medicaid health insurance claim form required by the Centers for Medicare and Medicaid Services (CMS) of the US Department of Health and Human Services. Private health insurance plans use the CMS-1500 form as well. The form was developed by the independent **National Uniform Claim Committee (NUCC)**. The CMS-1500 claim form is also used by all health care-related suppliers that send claims to Medicare-contracted claims administrators, as well as by all non-facility-oriented medical providers (e.g., a doctor's office, as opposed to a facility setting, such as a hospital).

DISABILITY BASED ON THE OCCUPATION OF THE INSURED

Disability insurers use two separate occupational definitions within disability insurance plans:

- **Own Occupation**: This definition asks if an employee can perform the duties of his or her current job. If not, he or she may qualify for benefits even if he or she can work in another job. Some policies might consider one's field to fall under the own occupation definition.
- **Any Occupation**: This definition asks if the insured can work in any occupation he or she is qualified for by education, training, or experience. If the insured can, then he or she usually cannot qualify for benefits, even if he or she must work in a lower-paying job or in a new field. This definition is much more detailed and, therefore, restrictive.

TIMELY CLAIMS PROCESSING

In most cases, health care providers send claims to a **clearinghouse** for processing. Once a claim is received by the clearinghouse, the claim is checked for errors and formatted correctly for easier processing by the insurer. Then, the clearinghouse submits the claim electronically to the insurer and sends a duplicate copy back to the provider.

The insurer receives the claim, evaluates it, and may request more information from the provider if there is any ambiguity regarding the services provided. The insurer then completes the processing of the claim and prepares an **explanation of benefits (EOB)** for both the insured and the provider. The EOB provides a detailed summary of how the claim was paid, including:

- The date of service (DOS)
- Procedure performed and its diagnostic code
- Provider's charge or billed amount
- Insured's financial responsibility (e.g., copays, deductibles, coinsurance, etc.)
- Final amount paid by the insurer to the provider

The final step in claims processing is when the insurer sends the payment to the provider. The EOB is usually sent to the provider attached to a check for payment of the claim or a statement regarding the electronic payment submitted to the provider.

Each state defines their own **timely payment of claims requirement** for both paper and electronically filed claims. Generally, each state sets minimum claims processing requirements. For instance, states require that health insurers acknowledge electronically filed claims received within a defined timeframe, such as within 24 hours after receipt of the claim.

In addition to processing of claims, each state sets specific guidelines for:

- Contested claims
- Payment of claims
- Denial of claims

PHYSICAL EXAMINATION OR AUTOPSY

State insurance regulations typically allow insurers to conduct and provide coverage for physical examinations and autopsies of the insured. A typical **autopsy clause** stipulates that the insurer may perform an examination or autopsy of the insured at the insurer's expense if a claim is pending, unless prohibited by law.

LEGAL ACTIONS PROVISION

Many health insurance policies contain a **legal actions provision** that prohibits an insured from taking legal action or suing an insurer for a specific period of time because of a claim that is still pending. This timeframe is generally either 60 or 90 days from the date of proof of loss. This window of time allows the insurer the ability to conduct a claims investigation while the claim is in dispute. This helps the insurer be thorough and not rush unnecessarily in the adjudication of the claim or inaccurately process it without all necessary information.

CHANGING THE BENEFICIARY

Insureds can generally change the beneficiary on their life insurance policy at any time. However, the life insurance company may require that certain conditions are met prior to changing it. For example, if the insured made the beneficiary designation irrevocable, it means the beneficiary cannot be changed without that same beneficiary's consent. The policy itself will show definitively whether a beneficiary is irrevocable. The most efficient way for insureds to make a beneficiary change is to contact the life insurance agent, who will help fill out the appropriate documentation to complete the change.

ALTERNATIVE MEDICINE TREATMENTS

Alternative medicine treatment is a growing area of covered benefits under many health insurance policies. Insurance policies generally provide coverage for alternative medicine treatments if they are medically necessary for the insured and have been shown to work either through clinical trials or by having had their effectiveness documented in published, peer-reviewed medical journals.

The following are alternative medicine treatments that, if medically necessary, are sometimes covered by health insurance:

- Acupuncture
- Chiropractic care
- Biofeedback

These benefits, along with others listed in a health insurance policy, are subject to applicable benefit plan limitations and exclusions.

EMPLOYER WELLNESS PROGRAMS

Wellness programs have become an increasingly popular means to achieve greater employee health and reduce an employer's health care costs. Wellness programs are offered either by an insurer to its enrollees or by an employer to its employees. Wellness programs usually have a goal of improving the participants' fitness and to promote a healthier lifestyle.

Wellness programs can offer a wide range of perks, including:

- Gym memberships
- Preventative health screenings
- Dietary counseling
- Smoking cessation
- Pedometers for walking
- Weight loss programs
- Diabetic maintenance programs

Wellness programs often promote participation through financial incentives, including reducing the insured's health insurance premiums, gift cards, cash payments, or retail discounts

INSURING CLAUSE

Every insurance policy contains an insuring clause or insuring agreement, which is a general statement of the assurances made by the insurer to the insured. In the insuring clause, the insurance company says that it will provide coverage for claims in the event of an insured loss as long as the insured continues to make premium payments and follows the policy conditions. Insurance, therefore, is the transfer of risk from the insured person to the insurance company. If a loss does not occur, the insured is out the premiums he or she has paid but retains the protection against future risks if the insured continues paying the premium.

CONSIDERATION CLAUSE

In an insurance contract, each party provides **consideration** to the other. In the insured's case, the premiums that he or she pays for the insurance coverage is the consideration the insured provides to the insurer. In the case of insurers, consideration refers to the money they pay on behalf of the insured to health care providers. Consideration means that each entity agreeing to an insurance contract offers some value, or consideration, for the relationship to work.

FREE LOOK PERIOD

Health insurers are generally required to allow policyholders a **free look period** of usually 15-30 days to provide them with a significant amount of time to be familiar with the terms and conditions of the policy. If during the free look period, the policyholder becomes uncomfortable with his or her decision, he or she can reverse the purchase decision without any further commitment. During the free look period, the policyholder can cancel the policy and get a premium refund, or he or she may ask the insurer for a change in benefits or features. The insured may also elect to purchase another policy altogether.

ELIMINATION PERIODS AND PROBATIONARY PERIODS

The **probationary period** is the timeframe at the beginning of an insurance contract during which an insured does not have coverage for services. The insured does not yet have active coverage and cannot file claims, yet the policy documents have been issued and coverage is technically effective. Often the probationary period for a new employee is 30, 60, or 90 days

In contrast, the **elimination period** is identified in disability and long-term care insurance contracts as the period of time that passes after the beginning of an injury but before the insurer begins paying benefits. The elimination period is occasionally also called a waiting period. During the elimination period the policyholder receives no benefits and is responsible for the payment for any care received. Once the elimination period is over, the insured receives full coverage and benefits in accordance with his or her policy.

The typical elimination period may be 30, 60, or 90 days. However, insureds typically get to select the elimination period they prefer. A longer elimination period means cheaper premiums, while a shorter elimination period means higher premiums.

MISSTATEMENT OF THE APPLICANT'S AGE

Age is one of the most important factors in how much an insurer decides to charge an individual for coverage. A misstatement of the applicant's age can mean a change of hundreds or more dollars per month in the premium owed. Insurers include a statement in most health and life contracts putting in place the action to be taken if a misstatement of age is discovered after the policy is in force. This is one of the most important provisions for individual health insurance policies. If it is found that the age of the applicant was accidentally misstated, the insurer can adjust premium payments and policy benefits. An insurer may decide to terminate insurance coverage of an individual who intentionally misstates his or her age on a life or health insurance application.

WAIVER OF PREMIUMS RIDER

Typically, the **waiver of premium rider** is purchased by the insured during the application process. This rider allows the insured, if he or she becomes disabled, to either temporarily or permanently postpone premium payments. During the period that premium payments are postponed, normal benefit coverage is still in force and available. Premium payments will be waived by the insurer for as long as the policyholder is unable to work because of a disability. Upon recovery, the policyholder restarts paying the premium, while owing no debt or extra premiums to the insurance company for the period he or she went without paying the scheduled premiums.

EXCLUSIONS

Insurers provide a detailed list of **exclusions** within health insurance policy documents to avoid ambiguity about what is not covered under their policies. Providing as much detail within an insurance policy concerning exclusions from coverage protects both parties from any later confusion regarding what procedures will not be covered. By avoiding ambiguity, the insurer is also attempting to avoid costly lawsuits that can arise if there are questions about what is covered and what is not.

There are many reasons health insurers have chosen to exclude certain conditions, surgeries, and treatments from coverage. Here are the most common reasons:

- Some might not be covered because they are deemed not medically necessary or are cosmetic treatments, such as chin implants and nose jobs.
- Others are restricted from coverage because of the exorbitant cost and financial impact on insurers, such as coverage for injuries related to acts of war (e.g., insurrections and terrorism).
- Other treatments, such as experimental cancer treatments, are excluded because they have yet to be proven effective by the medical community or approved by the US Food and Drug Administration.

Health insurance plans generally cover the cost of procedures if they are **reconstructive** (as opposed to purely cosmetic) in nature. For example, breast reconstruction after a mastectomy is covered, and this coverage is now actually required by law. A breast reduction may also be covered in cases where the patient experiences chronic back pain and the surgery is therefore medically necessary due to a health condition. The key to coverage is **medical necessity**. For instance, it is often not medically necessary to undergo a liposuction procedure. However, some cosmetic reconstructive surgeries following an accident or birth defect may be covered as well.

PREEXISTING CONDITIONS

In 2014, the ACA's consumer protections regarding **preexisting conditions** took effect. Because of ACA rules, health insurers can no longer take an individual's health or treatment history into account when deciding whether to sell them a health insurance policy. Insurers can no longer exclude coverage of preexisting conditions or deny coverage eligibility. In addition, insurers cannot charge an individual a higher premium versus other applicants simply because he or she has a preexisting condition. Regarding preexisting conditions and children's coverage, as part of the health reform law insurers can no longer deny health coverage to children younger than 19 because of a preexisting condition.

RECURRENT DISABILITY

An insured may experience a **recurrent disability**, which is a disability that results from the same cause or a related cause of a prior disability. Under the terms of a disability income policy, if an insured has a relapse, and it occurs within a specified time frame (usually 6-12 months) of the insured's return to the job, then this second incident is not considered a separate disability. Instead, it is considered a **continuation** of the first disability. Policies with recurrent disability benefits are helpful to the insured as the elimination period has already been satisfied and doesn't need to be met a second time.

COINSURANCE AND OUT-OF-POCKET MAXIMUM

Coinsurance is the percentage (e.g., 20 percent) of the billed amount that the insured is responsible for paying after the insured has already met his or her deductible. Typically, the higher the percentage of coinsurance for which an insured is responsible, the less expensive the monthly insurance premium is. To avoid the possibility of a catastrophic medical cost causing severe financial hardship for an insured, insurers apply a cap on the total medical costs an insured will pay in a year, which includes coinsurance, deductible amounts, and copays. This cap is called the **annual out-of-pocket maximum**. When the out-of-pocket maximum for the plan year has been reached, the insurer pays 100 percent of covered, eligible charges for the remainder of the plan year.

This cap is limited yearly by the ACA, and for 2022 the out-of-pocket maximum cannot be higher than $8,700 for an individual and $17,400 for a family.

DEDUCTIBLE

A health insurance **deductible** is how much the insured must pay before the insurer begins covering a portion of the costs. If a health insurance policy has a $500 deductible, the insured is responsible for the first $500 of charges billed by health care providers. After the deductible is met, the insurer will provide payment based on the terms and conditions of the policy. Premiums do not count toward the deductible, and copays generally do not count either.

Usually, a health insurance policy has one deductible and coinsurance amount for services received through an in-network provider and another (higher) deductible and coinsurance amount for services received through an out-of-network provider.

ACA-qualified health plans do not require the insured to pay anything, including copays and deductible amounts, for preventative care treatments. In other words, insurers pay 100 percent of these costs.

COPAY

A **copayment** or **copay** is a defined flat fee for services that insureds are expected to pay upon receiving a covered service. Copayments are typically required for specific services the insured receives, such as office visits or prescription drugs.

Copayments are technically another form of coinsurance that is based on a flat fee rather than a percentage. They are set dollar amounts such as $10, $15, or $25, depending on the medical service received. Copays paid by the insured generally do not count towards the deductible or coinsurance amounts.

DETERMINING ELIGIBLE EXPENSES FOR REIMBURSEMENT

Expenses eligible under most health insurance contracts are those detailed in the policy's **schedule of benefits** section. These are the policy terms that the insurer must adhere to in paying the insured's health insurance claims. Under traditional health insurance coverage, these costs run the gamut from a simple routine physical to laboratory tests and X-rays, to emergency room care or an outpatient surgical procedure. Eligible treatments covered by health insurance policies vary widely depending on the level and type of health insurance coverage purchased.

Increasingly, insurers are expanding coverage offered in health insurance plans to include alternative care and treatments, such as acupuncture and biofeedback. For alternative medicine and treatments, the insurer often covers a smaller portion of the charges compared to more traditional treatments.

PRE-AUTHORIZATIONS AND PRIOR APPROVAL REQUIREMENTS

Most commonly, pre-authorization, precertification, and prior authorization (often used interchangeably) refer to the process through which insurers require their insureds to gain preapproval for costly medical services and treatments. Pre-authorization allows the insurer an opportunity to review and validate that the planned treatment is the most cost-effective and is medically necessary. Insurance companies may require pre-authorization for a variety of health services like:

- Prescription drugs
- Diagnostic testing
- Medical devices
- Medical procedures

Pre-authorization generally includes a review of the doctor's medical notes and any applicable lab results or X-rays that may give insight to the insured's need for the treatment.

During the pre-authorization process, health insurance companies can require that patients meet certain criteria in advance of the planned treatment. For example, the insurance carrier will want to be sure the insured plans on using an in-network provider so that the medical service is performed at a discounted rate.

USUAL, REASONABLE AND CUSTOMARY (UCR) CHARGE LIMITS

The term **usual, reasonable, and customary (UCR)** is the amount paid for a medical claim in a geographic area based on what similar providers in the same area typically charge for the same or equivalent medical treatment. Insurance companies use UCR information to determine what reimbursement rate they should set for that specific service item in that geographic area. Often the UCR amount is used by insurance companies to set fee schedules when insureds see out-of-network providers for their health care needs.

LIFETIME AND ANNUAL MAXIMUM BENEFIT LIMITS

With the enactment of the ACA, both lifetime and annual maximum benefit limits on health insurance plans were no longer allowed. In the past, health insurers were able to set a **lifetime maximum benefit limit** (e.g., $1 million or $5 million) on what they would spend for the insured's covered benefits during the entire time they were enrolled in that plan. Previously, insureds covered by plans with a lifetime coverage limit were then required to pay the cost of all care exceeding the limit.

The ACA also bans **annual maximum benefit limits** on coverage for all group and individual health insurance plans. Before the health care law, many health plans set an annual dollar limit on their yearly spending for an insured's covered benefits. Like with the lifetime maximum, insureds were expected to pay any claims that exceeded the carrier's annual maximum benefit amount.

MINIMUM PREMIUM FUNDING ARRANGEMENTS

As a compromise between fully insured and self-funding for group health insurance, a **minimum premium funding arrangement** is available for small and medium-sized employer health groups. The minimum premium funding arrangement is used by employers to provide a third, midrange alternative between an **administrative services only** (ASO or self-insured) way of financing health coverage and the traditional, fully insured model. This provision allows the employer some group cost savings as it withholds a portion of premium that it would otherwise pay for a fully insured plan and provides funds to reimburse claims as they are paid. There is a maximum monthly amount that employers are liable for in regards to employee claims that is dependent on how many employees are covered. After this amount has been reached in a month, the responsibility falls on the insurance company. This alternative allows greater cash flow for the employer, while adding ASO-like tax advantages. For self-funded groups, moving to minimum premium funding arrangements can also reduce monthly insurance premiums and provide greater protection against claim costs.

EVIDENCE OF INSURABILITY

In the past, applications for health insurance required applicants to submit **evidence of insurability**. Basically, this meant they were required to answer dozens of health-related questions about both their family and personal medical history. As part of the underwriting process, applicants would need to list things like:

- Height and weight
- Prescription medications
- Chronic medical health conditions
- Acute medical conditions treated within the previous two years

The underwriter would review the information then decide whether the insurer should offer the applicant health insurance.

Under the terms of the ACA, these questions are no longer allowed for ACA-qualified health plans, as individuals can no longer be turned down for health insurance due to preexisting conditions.

GUARANTEED INSURABILITY

The ACA made significant changes to guaranteed issue laws. Beginning in 2014, all individual and group health plans were required to be **guaranteed issue** policies. Guaranteed issue means that individuals applying for health insurance are guaranteed access to health insurance and cannot be turned down because of their current health or preexisting conditions. This means that individuals with a history of illness or injury, including cancer, diabetes, heart conditions, HIV/AIDS, transplants, or other conditions (e.g., pregnancy), can't be turned down for health coverage.

In the past, insurance companies might have applied preexisting condition exclusionary riders to a policy that covered the insured for all health care except the preexisting condition named on the rider. Carriers would only cover new illnesses or injuries diagnosed after the policy's effective date. For example, insurers would exclude any care related to a child's autism if it were diagnosed prior to the policy's effective date.

The ACA's guaranteed insurability rules govern all group and individual plans sold inside or outside the health insurance marketplace. Individual plans that were grandfathered in after ACA are exempt from this guaranteed insurability rule. Grandfathered plans are those that were in place on or before March 23, 2010.

DOUBLE AND TRIPLE INDEMNITY

Double indemnity is a life insurance clause or provision in which the company agrees to pay double the policy's stated benefit amount in the case of an accidental death.

Insurance companies can also offer **triple indemnity**. If this option is available, beneficiaries may receive three times the face amount of the policy if an accident is the insured's cause of death. Many insurance companies define the type of accidents that qualifies for the AD&D rider. Accidents are unexpected happenings, such as car accidents and plane crashes.

Although double and triple indemnity clauses cover accidental deaths, these causes of death are excluded:

- Suicide
- Murder or conspiracy by any beneficiaries of the policy
- Death caused by the insured's own gross negligence
- Death by natural causes, like heart disease and cancer

CANCELLABLE AND OPTIONALLY RENEWABLE POLICIES

Cancellable insurance policies have language that allows the insured or the insurer to terminate coverage at any time, not just at renewal. If the insurance company decides to cancel the plan, then it is required to give notice to the policyholder and refund prepaid premiums on a pro-rated basis. In other words, the insurance company would have to return to the insured any unearned premiums.

Cancellation does not allow the insurer to deny responsibility for paying current, credible claims that were incurred while the policy was in force.

Unlike insurance policies that are cancellable, **optionally renewable policies** are plans that the insurer can choose, at renewal time, to cancel.

NONCANCELLABLE AND GUARANTEED RENEWABLE POLICIES

A **noncancellable insurance** policy has many advantages for the insured versus many other insurance policies because with noncancellable insurance, the insurer is not permitted to ever increase the premium, cancel the policy, or reduce the benefits if the policyholder continues to keep the coverage active. So, when the insured makes his or her first premium payment for the policy, he or she is assured that that premium amount will be the same over the entire life of the policy. Noncancellable policies are often disability or life insurance plans.

Noncancellable insurance policies are not exactly the same as **guaranteed renewable policies** because the latter only ensure that the insurer has to continue coverage as long as the insured pays his or her premiums. They do not ensure that the premiums stay at the same rate. Some guaranteed renewable policies may increase in premium, while noncancellable policies will not.

GUARANTEED RENEWABLE

Buying and renewing health insurance coverage isn't a simple exchange. One of the ACA rules that applies to health insurance companies is guaranteed renewability. This rule prevents companies from refusing to renew a policy when an insured becomes ill or develops a serious health condition. Guarantee renewability allows the policyholder to continue renewing the policy without changes to the contract terms being made by the insurer. The only condition an insurer can invoke to not renew a policyholder's coverage is if the insurer does not renew all similar policies of that kind across the board. In the case of an individual policy, the insurer may not add or delete provisions in the policy that may result in the insured's policy being canceled.

CONDITIONALLY RENEWABLE AND OPTIONALLY RENEWABLE

Insurance policies that are cancellable, optionally renewable, and conditionally renewable provide a great deal of leverage to the insurer versus the insured. These policies give the insurer the ability to install specific requirements on the insured that, if not adhered to, can allow the insurer to terminate the policy. The insured has no ability to impose anything similar on the insurer. These insurance plans can be cancelled at any point if conditions laid out in the contract are not met. If it desires, the insurer may also decide to increase the policy's premium.

A **conditionally renewable policy** allows an insurance company to end the coverage if one or more stipulations set forth in the contract occur. These stipulations are usually related to the insured reaching a particular milestone, such as reaching a set age, and again places all the decision-making and rulemaking with the insurer. When a policy has **optional renewability,** it means that the insurer may end the policy at its anniversary date or when the premium payment must be paid.

RENEWAL OF GROUP HEALTH INSURANCE PLANS

For group health insurance, the employer determines when the **group's renewal period** will happen. Renewals typically occur once per year. Most insurers do not allow groups to renew midyear without going through financial underwriting. At renewal time, the employer will review and determine, perhaps with its insurance agent's assistance, what and how many health plans it will offer and when it will allow employees to sign up for coverage. During the group's **open enrollment period**, the employer will let its employees know about the renewal process, the plan choices available, and allow employees to begin signing up for coverage.

LATE ENROLLEE

A **late enrollee** is an eligible employee who did not previously sign up for health coverage during the initial enrollment period. Instead, late enrollees sign up for their employer's group health plan during the next open enrollment period, unless the employer offers a special enrollment period. The open enrollment period usually occurs at the plan's anniversary and allows just about anyone to enroll so long as he or she meets the employer's guidelines.

Health Policy Revisions, Clauses, and Riders Chapter Quiz

1. Which of the following states that all pieces of the agreement between insurer and insured are found in the contract, and also keeps the insurance company from making arbitrary changes to the policy?

   a. Entire contract clause
   b. Incontestability clause
   c. Insuring clause
   d. Consideration clause

2. When did exclusionary riders become prohibited for all health insurance coverage?

   a. 2006
   b. 2010
   c. 2014
   d. 2018

3. Which of the following is required by state law and mandates that the insured provide information to the insurance company concerning a covered loss as soon as possible?

   a. Proof of loss provision
   b. Notice of claim provision
   c. Grace period provision
   d. Legal actions provision

4. Who developed the CMS-1500 form?

   a. US Department of Health and Human Services
   b. Independently contracted health care suppliers
   c. Centers for Medicare and Medicaid Services
   d. National Uniform Claim Committee

5. What does EOB stand for?

   a. Eligibility of beneficiaries
   b. Evidence of billing
   c. Entire occupational burden
   d. Explanation of benefits

6. Which of the following is one of the most important provisions for individual health insurance policies, and allows the insurer to adjust premium payments and policy benefits when applicable?

   a. Coordination of benefits provision
   b. Double indemnity provision
   c. Misstatement of age provision
   d. Minimum premium funding provision

7. What term is used to refer to the percentage of the billed amount that the insured is responsible for paying after the insured has already met their deductible?

   a. Expenses
   b. Copayment
   c. Out-of-pocket maximum
   d. Coinsurance

8. Which of the following do insurance companies utilize to determine what reimbursement rates they should set for a specific service item in a geographic area?

    a. Fee schedules
    b. Usual, customary, and reasonable (UCR) information
    c. Lifetime and annual maximum benefit limits
    d. Preexisting conditions

9. What policy type ensures that the insurer has to continue coverage as long as the insured pays his or her premiums, but does not guarantee that the premiums stay at the same rate?

    a. Guaranteed renewable policies
    b. Conditionally renewable policies
    c. Noncancellable insurance policies
    d. Optionally renewable policies

10. Which of the following would be covered by double and triple indemnity clauses?

    a. Suicide
    b. Accidental death
    c. Death by natural causes
    d. Murder or conspiracy by any beneficiaries of the policy

Social Insurance

MEDICARE PART A AND B (ORIGINAL MEDICARE)

Original Medicare covers two specific medical categories:

- **Medicare Part A** covers facility care, such as inpatient hospital stays and services, skilled nursing, nursing home care, hospice care, walkers and wheelchairs, and home health services. Part A also covers the cost of blood used during a blood transfusion when you are a patient at a facility.
- **Medicare Part B** covers preventative services and medically necessary services provided at a clinical office visit. Here are examples of medically necessary services that Part B covers:
  - Electrocardiograms (ECGs)
  - Medical equipment
  - Blood transfusions in an outpatient setting
  - Screenings for cancer, diabetes, and depression
  - Ambulance and emergency department services
  - Influenza and hepatitis B vaccinations
  - Some prescription drugs, eyewear prescriptions, and diabetes supplies

If an individual is eligible and covered by both Medicare and Medicaid, Medicaid is always the payer of last resort as Medicare takes the lead over Medicaid. However, if Medicare doesn't provide coverage for a specific item, Medicaid may provide that benefit if the item falls within Medicaid program coverage criteria.

MEDICARE PART C (MEDICARE ADVANTAGE PLANS)

Medicare Advantage (MA) Plans, also called **Medicare Part C,** are private health plans for Medicare participants. The private insurance companies that offer Medicare Part C plans are contracted by the federal government to provide Medicare benefits, essentially taking the place of Original Medicare. As stipulated by their federal contracts, Medicare Advantage Plans are usually required to cover at least the same amount of health care services as Original Medicare. Some of these plans provide additional coverage beyond what's included with Original Medicare. Those extra benefits often include:

- Prescription drug coverage
- Vision
- Dental
- Hearing benefits

Under a Medical Advantage Plan, some services may not be covered in all facilities or provider settings.

MEDICARE SUPPLEMENT PLANS

Medicare supplement insurance plans, also called **Medigap,** help pay for some of the out-of-pocket costs that Original Medicare doesn't cover. Medicare supplement plans are offered by private insurance companies and help provide additional coverage to the coverage already provided through Medicare Parts A and B. For instance, enrollment in Medicare Part B provides coverage for 80 percent of physician charges. If an individual purchases a Medicare supplement plan, it generally complements Original Medicare so that the two combined provide complete

77

coverage; the supplemental plan pays the remaining 20 percent of health care charges if the provider accepts **Medicare assignment**. A provider that does not accept Medicare assignment can charge up to 15% additional costs beyond Medicare's cost assignment. For Medicare Part A, supplement policies cover the Medicare Part A deductibles and coinsurance to effectively cover most, if not all, related expenses with the combination. Of course, Medicare participants that purchase a Medicare supplement must pay the Medicare premium out-of-pocket.

MEDICARE PART D

To receive **Medicare Part D** (prescription drug coverage), enrollees must sign up with a plan managed by a private insurer. Individuals have options and can choose either a **prescription drug plan (PDP)** or a Medicare Advantage Plan. A PDP plan adds Medicare Part D benefits to Original Medicare coverage. Unlike Medicare supplement plan premiums, the cost of Medicare Part D benefits is largely based on the enrollee's income. If income exceeds a benchmark, then that individual may pay more than a senior with a lower income.

Each Medicare PDP must give at least a standard level of coverage that is set by Medicare. PDPs set their approved drug lists (called a **formulary**) and categorize the drugs on the list into different tiers. There can be three different tiers (or levels), as well as a specialty tier. Members will pay a different co-payment amount depending on which tier their medication falls into. For example, generic drugs are usually assigned to Tier 1 and have the lowest copayment amount. Drugs in the specialty tier are usually very high-cost medications, and members will pay the highest copayment for these drugs.

When an individual becomes eligible for both Medicare and Medicaid, he or she is automatically enrolled in a Medicare Part D Prescription Drug Plan to ensure he or she doesn't miss a day of coverage.

For individuals who have dual eligibility, coverage under both Medicare and Medicaid, Medicare Part D prescription coverage takes precedence and replaces Medicaid in paying for most prescription drugs. This means most of an individual's drug costs will be paid for by Medicare instead of Medicaid.

WAITING PERIOD FOR MEDICARE ELIGIBILITY

When an individual becomes eligible for **Social Security Disability Insurance (SSDI) benefits**, that individual also gains eligibility for Medicare after a **24-month qualifying period**. During this qualifying period for Medicare, it is possible that the beneficiary may still have health care access through coverage via a former employer, or through COBRA continuation. Per the Social Security Administration, one month is counted for each month of disability benefit entitlement. Months in previous periods of disability may be counted towards the 24-month Medicare qualifying period if the new disability meets any of the following criteria:

- It begins within 60 months after the termination month of the worker's receiving disability benefits
- It begins within 84 months after the termination of disabled widows' or widowers' benefits or childhood disability benefits
- The current disabling impairment is the same as, or directly related to, the impairment which was the basis for the previous period of disability benefit entitlement.

MEDICAID

Medicaid is a federal and state-sponsored program that provides free or low-cost health care for some low-income:

- Individuals, including the elderly and disabled
- Families
- Children
- Pregnant women

Because their funding comes from both the federal government and state governments, Medicaid programs must follow federal guidelines, but coverage and costs vary by state. Some Medicaid programs pay for care received directly. Others use private contracted administrators or insurance companies to administer Medicaid benefits. Under the ACA, states had the option to expand coverage to additional persons beyond the standard Medicaid criteria and in accordance with federal guidelines.

ELIGIBILITY

The ACA created a national Medicaid **minimum eligibility level** of 138% of the **federal poverty level guideline (FPL)** for nearly all Americans under age 65. Childless adults make up a large percentage of this Medicaid population expansion. This means that the ACA applicant must meet the FPL guideline to qualify for a qualified health plan via the ACA exchange. If the applicant makes less than the FPL guideline, he or she is viewed as making too little to comfortably afford the least expensive ACA plan available within their state. If the applicant lives in a state that expanded Medicaid eligibility criteria to accept such ACA applicants, the individual will have his or her ACA application referred to the state's Medicaid program.

Household Size	2022 FPL Household Income
1	$13,590
2	$18,310
3	$23,030
4	$27,750
5	$32,470
6	$37,190
7	$41,910
8	$46,630
9+	Add $4,720 for each additional person

This Medicaid eligibility expansion became effective in 2014. As of 2022, 12 states have elected not to expand Medicaid coverage under the ACA.

PRIMARY AND SECONDARY PAYERS

Coordination of benefits (COB) is a term used when an insured is enrolled in two or more health insurance plans. The two insurers share information and coordinate benefits to make sure extra dollars are not unknowingly paid for the insured's medical care. The insurance industry has developed rules to determine which plan pays primary, secondary, and tertiary. For example, if both spouses are employees on their respective insurance plans, their primary coverage is through their employer, and the secondary coverage is then through the spouse's employer.

The birthday rule is used to decide how dependent children are covered by the two health plans. The rule is used if the parents are married, not separated, or have a joint custody order that does

not assign health coverage responsibility. Under the **birthday rule**, the primary payer is the parent whose birthday comes first during the calendar year. If both parents have the same birthday, the plan that has provided coverage longer is the primary payer.

OBTAINING SOCIAL SECURITY BENEFITS FOR RETIREMENT

When Americans work and pay Social Security taxes, they earn credits towards Social Security benefits. The number of credits individuals need to get retirement benefits depends on when they were born. For those born after 1929, they must have 40 credits to be eligible for retirement benefits. You can earn up to four credits per year, so you need a minimum of 10 years of working. If a person stops working before obtaining enough credits to qualify for benefits, the credits they have earned will remain on his or her Social Security record. If the individual returns to work later, he or she can add more credits to qualify. When an individual retires, his or her Social Security benefit is calculated by a complex formula that takes into account the earnings gained over one's lifetime,

BECOMING ELIGIBLE FOR SOCIAL SECURITY BENEFITS DUE TO A DISABILITY

The Social Security and Supplemental Security Income disability programs provide disability benefits and services to millions of disabled Americans. These two programs have similarities:

- Both are administered by the Social Security Administration
- Both provide needed benefits (specifically income) that aid vulnerable populations
- To gain access to benefits under each program the individual must have a disability and medically determinable impairments.

Social Security Disability Insurance (SSDI) pays benefits to the beneficiary and to certain members of his or her family, based on whether the individual is insured or has minor or disabled children when the insured became disabled. This is generally only for those who have worked and paid into Social Security, otherwise known as an "earned benefit". The Social Security Administration usually determines who qualifies for SSDI by establishing the amount of "work credits" earned by the individual. A credit is earned for each fiscal quarter the individual paid into Social Security; 20 out of the last 40 fiscal quarters are required to qualify (this is essentially 5 out of the last 10 years).

Supplemental Security Income (SSI) is a federal income supplement program funded by general tax revenues (not Social Security taxes). Its purpose is to aid aged, blind, and disabled persons who have little or no income regardless of work history or Social Security payments.

Social Insurance Chapter Quiz

1. As stipulated by federal contracts, which of the following is usually required to cover at least the same amount of health care services as Original Medicare, essentially taking the place of Original Medicare?

   a. Medicare Part A
   b. Medicare Part B
   c. Medicare Part C
   d. Medicare Part D

2. Medicare supplement insurance plans are also called:

   a. Medigap
   b. Medicare Advantage Plans
   c. Medicare assignments
   d. Medicare Part D

3. What are the costs of Medicare Part D benefits largely based on?

   a. Original Medicare rates
   b. The enrollee's income
   c. Medicare premiums
   d. Supplemental insurance coverage

4. What does COB stand for?

   a. Case only benefits
   b. Calculated, organized, and basic
   c. Coverage opportunity benchmark
   d. Coordination of benefits

5. Which of the following is NOT true of both the Social Security and Supplemental Security Income disability programs?

   a. Both provide needed benefits that aid vulnerable populations
   b. Both are administered by the Social Security Administration
   c. Both are funded by Social Security taxes
   d. To gain access to benefits the individual must have a disability and medically determinable impairments

Other Health Insurance Concepts

TOTAL DISABILITY

When an insured receives benefits under a disability income insurance policy, the individual must meet the criteria for either total disability or partial disability as defined by the policy. Most companies define **total disability** in two stages. The individual is deemed to be totally disabled if the disability does not allow him or her to perform the basic duties of his or her specific occupation. However, at the end of a defined period (usually within two years of becoming disabled), the individual is considered totally disabled only if he or she cannot perform any job that matches the individual's specific education, experience, and training.

PARTIAL AND RESIDUAL DISABILITY

An individual is considered **partially disabled** if the disability prevents him or her from performing one or more, but not all, primary tasks of his or her work; limits the amount of time or specified number of hours the individual is able to work; or causes his or her income to be reduced. With a partial disability benefit, the individual is compensated for the time lost on the job as well.

Residual disability benefits, comparatively, are based on a reduction or loss of an individual's earning power. Under this scenario, the disability income insurance benefit is graduated and equal to the earning power the insured has lost. If the individual's income loss is 70 percent because of the disability, the individual will receive 70 percent of the total disability benefit while he or she remains disabled. Certain restrictions may apply to different policies in terms of maximum benefit payout or capped percentage losses.

OWNER'S RIGHTS

The owner of an insurance policy is the one who has the rights stipulated in an individual health policy, which includes a death benefit. The **owner's rights** include the ability to name a beneficiary, if applicable. If the policy allows the beneficiary designation to be revoked, the insured may make a change of beneficiary whenever the insured chooses. When the beneficiary is revocable, the policyowner may also choose to make other policy changes without needing to gain the beneficiary's approval.

CHILDREN'S BENEFITS VS. ADULT BENEFITS

Typically, there are few differences between the benefits available to children and adults under the same health insurance policy. However, there are different preventive care visits and services available to children. These preventive services include immunizations and well-child appointments.

Often these preventive services dedicated for children are covered by insurers without requiring the insured to pay a copay or coinsurance that otherwise are required for similar diagnostic office visits and services.

ORDER OF BENEFIT DETERMINATION

The order of benefit determination rules, within health insurance policies, provide the order in which each health insurance policy will administer and pay claims. Coordination of benefits (COB) requires multiple insurers to share information and coordinate benefits. Carriers strive to coordinate benefits so that provider payments do not exceed 100 percent of the total allowable expense.

The plan that reviews and has the first responsibility for paying the claim is termed the primary plan. The primary plan is required to pay benefits in compliance with its specific policy terms. After the primary plan pays all claims in accordance with the contract terms, the secondary plan and tertiary plan will each pay the remaining claim amount due according to each of their policy terms.

IDENTIFYING PRIMARY AND CONTINGENT HEALTH INSURANCE BENEFICIARIES

The **primary beneficiary** is the individual(s) a policyholder selects to receive the death benefit paid when the insured dies. A **contingent beneficiary** is the individual or group of individuals that receives the death benefit if the primary beneficiary is no longer alive or able to receive the policy payout. The contingent beneficiary is basically a backup or replacement. Insureds can designate more than one primary or contingent beneficiary and will, therefore, need to assign percentages of the death payment to each named beneficiary. Most life insurance policies allow the policyholder to make changes to the primary beneficiaries and contingent beneficiaries, unless the insurance plan clearly states the beneficiaries are irrevocable.

KEEPING INSUREDS FROM PROFITING THROUGH EXCESSIVE HEALTH INSURANCE COVERAGE

The coordination of benefits clause is now a uniform provision for virtually all health insurance policies. This provision determines how duplicate coverage is administered when an insured or dependent has coverage under two different policies.

- The primary plan will pay its full, normal benefits—no more, no less. The primary plan is ordinarily the one in which the insured is the employee, and the secondary plan is usually the one where the insured is a dependent.
- The secondary plan will normally pay what is remaining of the total medical bill for services it allows under the policy, up to the maximum amount it would have paid if it were the sole insurance company for the patient.

Through this process, the insured will have health care expenses paid in full by the combination of the two health plans but will not receive more than the total amount due. If both health plans exclude a service under the policy, the service will not be covered, and the insured may have to pay that amount out-of-pocket.

OCCUPATIONAL BASED COVERAGE VS. NON-OCCUPATIONAL BASED COVERAGE

Most individuals in the United States gain health insurance coverage through their employer. Generally, the smaller the business, the less likely it is to offer employees insurance coverage.

Self-employed individuals and those who work for employers not offering insurance usually access health insurance through the **individual health insurance market**. Access to individual health insurance is now more widely available because of the Affordable Care Act. Individuals and their families may even be eligible for financial subsidies for coverage depending on their household income.

DIFFERENT WAYS IN WHICH INSURANCE PREMIUMS ARE TAXED

In an individual disability insurance plan, as long as policyholders pay premiums with after-tax dollars, the benefits received are not taxed. In group health insurance, if the employer gives its employees a lump sum amount to use for their health insurance premiums or for other health care purposes, that amount is tax free as long as the employee maintains a minimum essential health insurance coverage (MEC) plan.

Unlike health insurance premiums, however, policyholders are not allowed to deduct premiums paid as a medical expense for an individual disability insurance policy. Because disability insurance benefits include income replacement, rather than paying for health care services, it is not a deductible medical expense.

MANAGED CARE

Managed care is a health care delivery method that seeks to control the costs of health care services while improving health care quality. **Managed care organizations** typically contract with a group of selected providers and discourage access to providers outside of that group. To encourage the use of contracted providers, the managed care organization provides fewer benefits for services from noncontracted providers.

Managed care organizations include:

- Health maintenance organizations (HMO)
- Preferred provider organizations (PPO)
- Point-of-service plans (POS)

CASE MANAGEMENT

Case management is the means used by health insurers to improve the coordination of services on behalf of an individual person with a severe illness or chronic health condition when there are many different health care providers treating the individual. Case management for health insurance companies is typically performed by health care professionals with nursing experience to assure expert involvement. By managing medical care more closely, case managers ensure that health care services are efficient, effective, and appropriate for each individual's health and circumstances.

WELLNESS PROGRAMS

Wellness programs are seen by employers as a means of empowering employees to improve their health and quality of life. Some wellness programs that employers offer are:

- Health fairs
- Health education
- Medical screenings
- Health coaching
- Weight management programs
- Smoking cessation
- Health club memberships
- Fitness programs
- Fitness contests

Other wellness program initiatives can include flexible work schedules to allow for exercise, as well as financial incentives for improved health markers (e.g., cholesterol and weight). By creating a healthier workforce, employers are also hoping to see reduced health insurance premiums as a result.

WORKERS' COMPENSATION

Workers' compensation provides benefits for workers who are injured while working or become ill as a direct result of their work. The injuries or illnesses may be either physical or mental. Workers' compensation laws cover those in **industrial employment**, a term that encompasses those working in factories and construction, and other types of workers, such as office and retail workers. However, workers' compensation is regulated by states, and each state has its own exclusions when it comes to coverage. For example, several states exclude domestic workers (e.g., nannies and maids), agricultural workers, and those who work for religious organizations. Often these types of workers are excluded only if they work part time. Also, some states exempt businesses with fewer than five employees from having to cover their workers. However, while certain groups are exempted depending on a state's workers' compensation laws, employers may still decide to voluntarily cover their employees if they choose.

Most workplace injuries are covered under workers' compensation insurance programs through employers. Benefits are generally available following a waiting period, which is usually seven days. Benefits though are usually paid, depending on state requirements, retroactively if the injury keeps the employee out of work longer than 14 days.

Employers are required to contribute funds for workers' compensation benefits through regular premiums to an insurance company or to a state fund. Business owners who fail to provide workers compensation coverage may be subject to civil and sometimes even criminal penalties. Employers must provide benefits through one of the following:

- A private insurance company
- Adequate self-insurance
- A nonprofit state compensation insurance fund

The employer is responsible for injuries that employees experience during their work hours without regard to who is the responsible party. Typically, the injured employee must be compensated regardless of whether or not the employer was negligent, the employee was careless, or the accident was unavoidable.

Though workers' compensation laws may differ among states, there are **common benefits** that all employers can expect to receive. In most situations, injured employees receive benefits (both long term and short term) no matter who was responsible for their injuries.

Workers' compensation insurance generally covers health care services including:

- Rehabilitation from the injury or illness
- Costs for retraining
- Compensation for any permanent injuries
- Replacement income
- Benefits to survivors of workers who are killed on the job

In many states, employees are barred from suing their employer for a workplace injury as long as the employer has the proper workers' compensation coverage available.

SUBROGATION

Subrogation is the process used by insurers to investigate and determine if a third party is responsible for the health care coverage of an injury caused to one of their policyholders. If the insurer's investigation reveals the other party is responsible for the claim, the insurance carrier has the legal right to seek reimbursement from the responsible party. Subrogation comes into play often when it comes to health insurance and auto insurance.

For instance, an insured of XYZ Insurance goes to the emergency room with a broken ankle. The insurance company receives no notice that the injury was sustained in an auto accident. Two months later, XYZ insurance learns that the insured's car was hit by another driver and this resulted in the broken ankle. XYZ insurance begins the subrogation process of reaching out to the other driver's auto insurance provider for reimbursement of the policy benefits paid under the insured's health insurance plan.

ACCOUNTABLE CARE ORGANIZATIONS (ACO)

Accountable care organizations (ACO) are recommended by the ACA to reduce health care costs by encouraging doctors, hospitals, clinics, and other health care providers to improve member care coordination. The ACO care model works with the Medicare program and is an example of an innovative model providing bonuses to participating providers who improve health care efficiency and achieve improved health care outcomes for patients. When ACOs save money and meet their quality-of-care goals, they can keep a portion of the savings.

Other Health Insurance Concepts Chapter Quiz

1. What type of benefits are based on a reduction or loss of an individual's earning power?

    a. Total disability benefits
    b. Residual disability benefits
    c. Secured disability benefits
    d. Recurrent disability benefits

2. Which of the following is now a uniform provision for virtually all health insurance policies, and determines how duplicate coverage is administered?

    a. Coordination of benefits clause
    b. Point-of-service planning
    c. Guaranteed insurability provision
    d. Primary and contingent benefits

3. Which of the following does NOT fall underneath managed care organizations?

    a. Point-of-service plans (POS)
    b. Health maintenance organizations (HMO)
    c. Accountable care organizations (ACO)
    d. Preferred provider organizations (PPO)

4. What is the means used by health insurers to improve the coordination of services on behalf of an individual person with a severe illness or chronic health condition when there are many different health care providers treating the individual?

    a. Combination plans
    b. Case management
    c. Wellness programs
    d. Subrogation

5. What is the process used by insurers to investigate and determine if a third party is responsible for the health care coverage of an injury caused to one of their policyholders called?

    a. Litigation
    b. Compensation
    c. Retaliation
    d. Subrogation

Field Underwriting Procedures

AGENTS AND BROKERS

It is important to understand the differences between an insurance broker and an insurance agent.

An insurance **agent** usually represents one specific insurance carrier. The positives of working with an insurance agent can be a lower rate, easier plan changes, and a closer working relationship with the insurer since the agent is the insurer's representative.

Meanwhile, an **insurance broker** works with multiple insurance carriers. The positive of working with a broker is a broker will provide the applicant with various policy options at different rates. The broker can offer a customer more coverage options than an insurance agent since the latter is usually limited to one carrier.

Salaries for agents and brokers are largely based on commissions so keeping clients happy and renewing their coverage is beneficial for both.

UNDERWRITING LIFE INSURANCE POLICIES

The underwriting process evaluates the risks presented to the insurer by applicants seeking life insurance coverage. If the life insurer did not have adequate applicant risk assessment processes and accepted every applicant without hesitation, it would likely incur heavy losses as it would be accepting high-risk applicants.

If each application is thoroughly investigated, there is also a low probability of insurance fraud. The insurer minimizes the risk of paying on fraudulent claims by closely reviewing each applicant's medical history, height-to-weight ratio, laboratory tests, and the insured's family health history, among many other health indicators. When an applicant is high-risk, a higher premium might be charged or the coverage could be decreased. In some cases, life insurance might be denied.

REQUIRED MEDICAL EXAM FOR LIFE INSURANCE COVERAGE

A comprehensive medical exam is often a key element in an insurer's risk assessment of a life insurance applicant. Medical exams offer real-time insights that are not always available through other means when evaluating an applicant's risk profile. Typically, insurance companies send a registered nurse or medical technician to the applicant's home or work, wherever he or she prefers, to collect specimens such as urine and blood and to evaluate the applicant's overall health. The insurer pays for this medical exam.

A medical exam allows the insurer to lessen its risk by generating detailed information on the applicant. A medical exam may also aide the underwriter in determining the applicant's health status and life expectancy. The results of the medical exam may also help the insurer in setting the new insured's premium rate.

MIB Group, Inc. (MIB) Report

MIB Group, Inc. (formerly the Medical Information Bureau) is an interchange of health information insurers refer to during the underwriting process. Insurance companies use MIB reports to assess insurance applicants and the risks they represent, catching errors, misstatements, and oversights offered within an individual's insurance application. Companies submit underwriting information to MIB, and that information can then be accessed by other underwriters. The information is coded and used exclusively by the insurance companies that are members. An individual's MIB record includes the medical status and conditions that might impact an individual's long-term health outlook.

An MIB report includes the following type of information:

- Medical impairments or conditions
- When the medical condition was treated and/or diagnosed
- The types of treatments the applicant received
- The source of the medical history
- The date of any previous life insurance applications

MIB gathers and obtains the materials presented with the applicant's consent. Insurance companies must use MIB information as a signal of potential discrepancies only; the information cannot be used as a stand-alone definitive source and must be verified through a secondary resource.

Fair Credit Reporting Act (FCRA)

The Fair Credit Reporting Act (FCRA) requires that an applicant be told if a consumer report is requested and be informed of the details of the possible investigation. It protects policyholder's privacy rights and helps to ensure that credit report information is valid when presented and available in credit reports. The FCRA seeks to promote the accuracy, fairness, and privacy of a patient's information. If a health insurer declines the application because of information learned from the applicant's credit report, the insurer is required to provide the applicant the name and address of the reporting agency they used.

Explaining Riders, Exclusions, and Rating Factors

Insurance documents are complex and often difficult to comprehend for the general public. A licensed insurance agent will take the time necessary to explain the insurance. A customer with a new policy that he or she does not understand is not a good foundation for an ongoing agent-client relationship. Agents and brokers need to ask questions of the insured to ensure that he or she understands the policy language and the coverage being purchased, as well as the premiums to be paid

How and When Policy Becomes Effective

The insurance agent accepts the initial premium at the time of the completed application and then issues to the applicant a **conditional receipt**. This conditional receipt (or binding receipt) makes coverage effective on either the date of application or the date of the medical examination, if one is required by the insurer.

If the initial premium is not paid to the insurance agent at the time of the application, the policy becomes effective at a later date, after the initial premium is paid.

If the premium had been paid at the time of application, but the conditional receipt was not given to the applicant, the policy would start instead when the policy is delivered. Coverage does not begin until both the policy is issued by the insurer and the premium payment is paid by the insured.

CERTIFICATE OF INSURANCE

The **certificate of insurance** is a document issued by an insurance company that serves as proof that the insurance coverage and its specific coverage provisions exists. Among the items included in the certificate of insurance are:

- The effective date of coverage
- The policy type purchased by the insured
- The policy's coverage terms, limitations, and exclusions

A certificate of insurance is often requested by attorneys during litigation where parties are disputing liability and coverage specifics. If, for example, coverage for a specific medical procedure is up for debate, a certificate of insurance may be requested to verify and determine whether the surgery is a covered benefit or a limitation or exclusion to the policy.

ADMINISTERING THE REPLACEMENT OF A LIFE INSURANCE POLICY

Replacing an existing life insurance or annuity policy is a complex process and may contain extra, unforeseen costs such as **acquisition costs** or **surrender costs**.

The agent or broker needs to aid the policyholder in carefully comparing the costs and benefits of the proposed replacement policy against the insured's existing policy. To assist with this process the agent could develop a document that shows a side-by-side comparison of the two policy's benefits, coverage, limitations, and costs.

ALEATORY CONTRACTS

An **aleatory contract** is an agreement in which both parties aren't expected to take any action until a triggering event occurs. For life insurance, the triggering event is death. For homeowners' insurance, a triggering event would be a house fire. This concept applies to all types of insurance coverage.

With life insurance policies, the risk of an insured's death is variable and uncertain. This fact can create an aleatory result. For example, if the insured dies unexpectedly shortly after the policy is issued, the beneficiary will most likely receive a death benefit payout that far exceeds the premiums paid towards the coverage.

In another example, the insurer of a health insurance policy may benefit greatly from premiums received for an insured that never files a medical claim. That means the insurance company is benefiting from the aleatory contract, but the insured is not since they have used zero of the policy's benefits.

EXECUTORY CONTRACTS

An executory contract is a contract in which both parties have obligations they need to fulfill before the contract can be fully executed at a later date. Life insurers only complete their obligation upon payment of the death benefit. This means the insurer's responsibilities remain unfulfilled until the processing and payment of a claim.

UNILATERAL CONTRACTS

A life insurance contract is deemed **unilateral** because the insurer is the only party required under the contract to perform its stated duties under the policy. On the other hand, the premium the insured pays for the coverage is a **consideration**, not a promise of performance. Life insurance is also unilateral because the insured's estate can sue the insurance company for failing to fulfill its promise paying the death benefit. In contrast, the insurance company cannot sue the living insured or the insured's estate for failure to make premium payments.

CONDITIONAL COVERAGE

Conditional coverage life insurance is coverage that commences at the time the customer signs the application. Upon receiving that first premium, the insurer issues a conditional receipt to the applicant. Therefore, the insured is conditionally covered by the insurance policy immediately—provided that the insurance company's underwriters approve the application. This process makes the policy active before the policy documents are issued, provided the applicant meets all the conditional requirements.

INSURABLE INTEREST

Insurable interest exists when an individual relies on a benefit (usually financial) from the person who is insured. Therefore, an individual possesses an **insurable interest** in the insured such that he or she would experience a financial hardship or burden should the insured pass away. To seek insurance on a person, an applicant for life insurance coverage must benefit more financially from the person continuing to live than the applicant would benefit from the insured passing on.

ADHESION CONTRACT

A life insurance policy is not the type of contract that is negotiated between equal parties. Instead, the contract is drafted by one party (the insurer) with no input or discussion from the other party (policyholder). The policyholder must either accept or reject the contract as is. The policyholder does not have the option of negotiating, revising, or deleting any of the document's content. This type of contract is called an adhesion contract. Due to the nature of this type of contract, courts generally interpret any ambiguity existing in an insurance contract in the policyholder's favor because of that unequal relationship. Courts have regularly ruled in the policyholder's favor by allowing reasonable expectations on the part of the policyholder (or the named beneficiaries), because the contract is prepared solely by the insurer without input from the policyholder.

WARRANTY

A warranty is a term contained in the policy that affirms the existence of certain facts or a statement that establishes that something the insured person has stated is true. An insurance contract is based on trust; each party trusts the other in the contract relationship to do and say what is stipulated in the contract. For the contract to be credible, an individual may need to provide proof that an assumption the insurer is making is valid. For example, a life insurance applicant must testify that he or she is not near death or terminally ill. Thus, the applicant is making a warranty regarding his or her good health. Therefore, if the insurer found that an applicant's warranty was not valid, it possesses the discretion to void the contract and not honor the insured's claim.

REPRESENTATIONS

Representations are the statements made by the insurance applicant on the application for insurance. The applicant's representations often are a direct response to questions posed within the application. For example, representations can include the applicant's age and birthdate, health history, and prescribed medications.

An insurance contract is **voidable** by the insurer if any representation is found to be false and was either material, relied upon by the insurer, or known to be false by the insurance applicant.

A **material representation** is a statement that gets someone to agree to a contract that the party would not have agreed to without that statement being made. An example might be if an applicant failed to mention that they have a chronic disease that they simply decided not to take medicine for. If the insurer knew the applicant had a chronic disease that may cause future health problems, the insurer may have decided not to issue the policy or issue it with different policy terms or a higher premium. This might be considered a material misrepresentation worthy of voiding the contract.

Field Underwriting Procedures Chapter Quiz

1. Which of the following is NOT usually true of an insurance broker?

    a. Insurance brokers represent one specific insurance carrier.

    b. Salaries for brokers are largely based on commissions.

    c. Insurance brokers will provide the applicant with various policy options at different rates.

    d. The broker can offer a customer more coverage options than an insurance agent.

2. Which of the following requires that an applicant be told if a consumer report is requested and be informed of the details of the possible investigation?

    a. Health Insurance Portability and Accountability Act

    b. Pension Protection Act

    c. Fair Credit Reporting Act

    d. USA Patriot Act

3. Which of the following statements is NOT true of MIB?

    a. MIB's information is coded and used exclusively by insurance companies that are members

    b. MIB Group, Inc. is an interchange of health information

    c. MIB information can be used as a stand-alone definitive source

    d. Insurance companies use MIB reports to assess the risks associated with applicants

4. What type of contract is drafted by one party with no power of input, discussion, negotiation, or revision being given to the other party?

    a. Aleatory contract

    b. Executory contract

    c. Unilateral contract

    d. Adhesion contract

5. Which of the following is a document issued by an insurance company that serves as proof that the insurance coverage and its specific coverage provisions exist?

    a. Conditional receipt

    b. Certificate of insurance

    c. Warranty of contract

    d. MIB report

6. Which of the following is a statement that gets someone to agree to a contract that the party would not have agreed to without that statement being made?

    a. Insurable interest

    b. Material representation

    c. Conditional coverage

    d. Warranty

Chapter Quiz Answer Key

Types of Life Policies

1. C: Increasing term life insurance has a death benefit that increases each year. It usually increases either by a certain percentage or a flat rate. Since the death benefit increases, the premiums cost more than level term life insurance, and the premiums can get more expensive throughout the years. Another type of term life insurance is decreasing term insurance in which premiums stay the same, but the death benefit decreases at a preset and steady rate. The philosophy behind this type is that a person's need for high levels of insurance lessen as he or she gets older as certain financial obligations lessen or get resolved, such as paying off a mortgage or student loans. Another term life insurance type is return of premium. These policies provide a return on the premiums paid by the insured if the term ends without a death benefit being paid out.

2. B: A single premium whole life (SPL) policy is, as its name implies, a whole life insurance plan with one large premium payment due at the time of issuance. The policy is fully paid up, and no further premiums are needed after that initial large payment. The SPL is fully guaranteed to remain paid up until the insured's death. A single premium whole life policy can also be referred to as a modified endowment contract (MEC). There are different laws regarding how withdrawals from the cash value in MECs are taxed versus every other type of permanent life insurance policy.

3. A: Variable whole life differs from traditional whole life in that the cash value is invested in various investment accounts picked by the insurance company, such as mutual funds, annuities, money market funds, etc. This differs from the low interest rate applied to the cash value in a traditional whole life policy that the insurer picks and is only altered annually. Variable whole life policies are riskier because the policy's cash value and death benefits can rise and fall depending on market forces and the investment's performance. If the policy's investments perform well, the death benefit and cash value are likely to increase, but if the market isn't very strong, then both the death benefit and cash value can decrease. However, there is a minimum guaranteed payout to the beneficiaries if the death benefit were to lose a lot of value. Because of the investment aspect, variable policies are considered a security. This means they are subject to federal securities laws, and an accompanying prospectus is required when they are sold.

4. C: Surrender charges are included by insurance companies to limit the number of withdrawals an annuitant can take over a set number of years from the beginning of the annuity. To do this, insurers may include a surrender charge on any withdrawals above an established threshold. These charges provide assurance to the insurer that it will receive some income if an annuitant decides to end or alter the policy.

5. D: Deposits into annuity contracts are typically inaccessible for a designated period. That means an annuity is viewed as being the opposite of a liquid asset, or rather illiquid. Annuities vary widely in their ability to be converted to cash.

Life Policy Riders, Provisions, Options, and Exclusions

1. B: A rider attaches added coverage to a life insurance policy over and above the simple death benefit as defined by the standard policy. Riders can either provide a free added benefit, or can be added to the base policy for an additional cost. A waiver of premium rider allows an insured to have his or her life insurance premiums forgiven if the insured incurs a disability that limits his or her

94

ability to earn a living. Without this rider, the inability to pay the insurance premium could lead to cancellation of the coverage. The premiums are waived for the length of the disability. Some insurers also allow insureds who develop a disability and who have the added waiver of premium rider to convert their term policies into permanent insurance policies.

2. D: Accidental death and dismemberment insurance policies are usually purchased as riders for life insurance or health insurance. In the case of life insurance, the AD&D rider provides a separate, additional benefit if the policyholder's death occurs due to an accident, often doubling the amount of the life insurance payout. Accidental death benefits are not paid for all accidental deaths; but there are some notable exclusions for inherently dangerous activities, such as a death that is the result of military service. Death or injury due to the insured's participation in illegal activities, self-inflicted injuries, or hazardous hobbies (e.g., skydiving, rock climbing, cliff diving, etc.), are also excluded. If an insured participates in these activities, the insurer may require the insured to pay a higher premium or have the activities excluded from coverage.

3. C: Life insurance carriers began offering return-of-premium riders on their term policies because traditional term policies only pay benefits when the insured dies. However, if the policyholder doesn't die before the term ends, this rider lets him or her regain all or part of the premiums he or she paid to the insurer over the policy's life. It also allows the insurer to use the paid premiums as an investment during the length of the term. Including this rider makes the premiums much higher than a term life insurance without it.

4. B: The central component at the heart of an insurance contract is what's termed the insuring clause provision, which contains details on the type and specifics of coverage issued by the insurer. This clause is the linchpin of the insurance policy because it details everything a life insurance policy accomplishes in protecting the insured. The insuring clause specifies that when an insured makes his or her premium payment, the company will provide a stated amount to the beneficiary or the insured as stipulated in the policy.

5. D: When included in a policy, the common disaster clause provides that if the insured and the designated beneficiary die simultaneously or due to the same common event, it is assumed that the beneficiary died first. This clause is helpful to streamline the death benefit payout, as it enables the policy proceeds to be paid to the contingent beneficiary and avoids having the policy proceeds be paid to the primary beneficiary's estate. If there is no contingent beneficiary named, then the proceeds are paid directly to the insured's estate.

6. A: Depending on the insurer, the following options are available for the mode of premium payment: annually, semiannually, quarterly, or monthly. Premium payment amounts are either:

- Level (as with ordinary life insurance): Usually this is a monthly, quarterly fixed, or defined payment schedule.
- Single payment (as with single premium whole life): The policy calls for a one-time lump sum premium payment.
- Graded premium (as with graded premium whole life): Premiums are set on either an increasing or decreasing payment schedule.
- Flexible premium (as with universal life): The insured can alter his or her premium payments as seen fit within policy guidelines, making payment options very flexible.

7. B: Reinstatement is the process of reinstalling a policy that's become lapsed due to nonpayment of premiums. In most cases, permanent life insurance contracts permit policyowners to reinstate a lapsed policy. Under this reinstatement provision, the policyowner will be responsible for paying back all outstanding premiums with interest. A reinstated policy usually starts a new contestable period (two years); however, it does not require a new suicide period.

8. A: Nonforfeiture options are available in permanent insurance contracts. In an insurance policy, a nonforfeiture provision states that the insured may receive all or some of the benefits or a partial refund on the premiums that have already been paid if the policy lapses because the insured neglects to make premium payments. Often, a nonforfeiture clause will only stay in effect for a set timeframe at the outset of the policy. The nonforfeiture clause may also only become active if the policy has been in force after a certain amount of time, per stipulations detailed in the contract.

9. D: If a deceased insured misrepresented his or her age, the face amount of the policy will be changed and reestablished to the amount that the premium would have bought at the insured's correct age at the time of purchase. The incontestability period does not apply to misstatements of age or gender. For example, if an insured claimed on the insurance application four years earlier to be 43 years old when in fact, he or she was 53 years old, the $250,000 policy purchased would be adjusted to a lower face amount in the event of his or her death. An overstatement of age will usually result in a refund of premium payment.

10. D: The following are standard settlement options available to life insurance beneficiaries:

- Lump-sum cash settlement: When receiving a lump-sum payment, the named beneficiary receives the entire policy face amount at once.
- Interest only: With this option, the beneficiary can get an interest-only limited benefit and defer the face amount to a later time he or she selects.
- Fixed period installments: With this option, the death benefit is distributed as equal monthly payments for the selected period until the entire face amount plus accrued interest is paid.
- Fixed amount installments: If this option is chosen, the beneficiary will receive monthly payments in the specified amount until the entire face amount plus accrued interest is paid.
- Life income options: If the beneficiary selects the life income option, they receive the proceeds of the policy as an annuity.

Completing the Application, Underwriting, and Delivering the Life Policy

1. C: A warranty is an essential condition upon which the insurer and insured agree for the contract to take effect. For instance, in a life insurance application, a warranty might be that the insured guarantees that he or she is not presently terminally ill or in hospice care. In contrast, a representation is not an essential condition of an insurance policy, but is simply the current information provided in the application. Representations within a life insurance application are statements made by the applicant that impact the insurer's decision to offer insurance. Types of representations within an insurance application include such things as a person's date of birth, a list of current medical conditions, or prescription drugs currently used by the insured. Representations could also include other facts such as the insured's height and weight at the time of the application. Still other representations would be factual answers to family health history questions, such as the ages when the insured's parents died and their causes of death.

2. D: When an application is complete, the agent and the applicant both sign it. The agent provides the insured a conditional receipt upon the applicant's payment of the first premium. This offers a window to the insurers to ultimately deny or approve the policy until it is determined if the insured meets the stands of insurability.

3. B: In the life insurance policy application process, the life insurer and agent are required to have the applicant sign a Health Insurance Portability and Accountability Act (HIPAA) disclosure acknowledgement. This disclosure informs the applicant that his or her personally identifiable health information will be protected and held strictly confidential by the insurer.

4. A: Insurance companies are susceptible to money laundering, and insurance agents, producers, and brokers play a key role in the insurance process. Thus, the USA Patriot Act established anti-money laundering (AML) requirements that require insurers and brokerages to include employee training on independent audits and policies to detect suspicious behavior and potential money laundering within insurance transactions. The anti-money laundering regulations enacted as part of the USA Patriot Act apply to the following insurance-related products:

- Permanent life insurance, other than group life insurance
- Annuity contracts, other than a group annuity contract
- Any other insurance product with features of cash value or investment

5. B: The federal Fair Credit Reporting Act (FCRA) mandates that insurers provide notices to applicants when they take an adverse action using information gleaned from consumer reports about the applicant. An adverse action is any action taken by the insurer because of information presented in the consumer report that negatively affects the situation of an applicant. For example, suppose an insurer reviews an applicant's credit history to decide whether the applicant can afford the insurance premiums. If the insurer finds a poor credit score during its review and thus gives the applicant a surcharge in addition to the regular insurance premium, which is an adverse action, the insurer must notify the applicant and give him or her a chance to dispute the information in the report.

6. C: Stranger-originated life insurance (STOLI) is the term used when a person applying for life insurance wants to locate a new insurance policy with a beneficiary who has previously not known the insured and does not have an insurable interest in the insured. These policies are on the fringe of questionable business practices and have come under scrutiny from insurance regulators and the industry in general, as they may conflict with state insurable interest laws. A STOLI transaction is not intended to be insurance protection but is rather intended to be an investment mechanism for the policy owner's beneficiaries.

Taxes, Retirement, and Other Life Insurance Concepts

1. C: An insurance underwriter's primary job function is to evaluate the risks and exposures of potential clients by looking at their medical history and other risk factors. Underwriters decide if the individual's risk is acceptable to the insurer, how much coverage he or she should be offered, and what the best premium rate should be. Underwriters ultimately are tasked with protecting insurers from bad risks and setting premium rates sufficiently high to be profitable for the insurance company.

2. A: Many life insurance policies include a conversion privilege clause that provides individuals with an opportunity to transition easily to individual life insurance coverage after leaving an employer where they had group life insurance coverage. With this provision, employees can effectively change a group life insurance policy into an individual policy without undergoing a medical exam or additional underwriting. With this conversion, the insurer extends coverage based on the employee's previous approval for coverage and maintains an actively insured person rather than losing a client.

3. B: An individual's Social Security benefit is calculated using a complex formula that gets you a number called the primary insurance amount (PIA). The PIA is how much you will receive in Social Security benefits if you elect to start receiving them at normal retirement age, which is 67 for people born in 1960 and after. A person is first eligible to start receiving benefits at 62; however, if you start receiving benefits before your normal retirement age, those benefits will not be your full PIA but a reduced amount that is determined by the Social Security Administration.

4. C: Overall, an average worker's Social Security benefit amount can generally be expected to be about 40 percent of his or her average lifetime earnings. The term worker applies to someone that has earned a total of at least 40 credits during his or her lifetime. Credits are earned when you work and pay Social Security taxes. You can earn up to four credits a year, so it usually takes 10 years to qualify for Social Security.

5. D: In group life insurance plans where premiums are paid by the employer, employees can receive coverage up to a $50,000 death benefit without incurring any tax liability. However, if coverage exceeds a $50,000 death benefit, employees are required to treat the excess cost of the life insurance premium as income and pay taxes on it.

Types of Health Policies

1. B: An insured gives a statement providing details about the illness or injury when he or she files a claim under a disability income insurance policy. This provides written acknowledgement to the insurer of the individual's claim for benefits. In analyzing the claim, the insurer often seeks to verify the insured's statement regarding the illness or injury by requesting an attending physician's statement (APS). This is completed by the insured's doctor and tells the insurer the circumstances surrounding the disability. The APS details the insured's medical history, health care plan, and how the disabling condition came to be.

2. C: Business overhead expense (BOE) insurance provides coverage for the owner should he or she become disabled. BOE is meant to cover the routine, normal overhead costs. Overhead expense coverage is not equivalent to personal disability insurance. A business overhead expense policy provides benefits for a shorter benefit period of about one to two years after a waiting period is completed. This coverage is useful in preventing a business from shutting down, being sold, or going into debt if the owner becomes disabled. These policies also work in circumstances where there is more than one owner. If the business is a partnership, each partner can obtain a BOE policy to provide protection for his or her individual share of the costs of running the business.

3. A: A basic hospital plan offers low-cost basic financial protection from large health care costs. This is a standalone policy that appeals to young and healthy individuals who do not require frequent medical services or could not otherwise qualify or afford major medical insurance. Also commonly referred to as a catastrophic plan, basic hospital insurance typically covers:

- Hospitalization and inpatient care
- Prescription drug coverage during inpatient treatment
- Surgery
- Other services performed on an outpatient basis (excluding prescription drugs)
- Emergency room services

4. A: Providers contracted with a health maintenance organization (HMO) do not receive traditional payment as each health care service is rendered. Instead, HMO physicians receive a capitated monthly rate up front to provide health care to enrolled members. Because physicians contracted with the HMO are paid a set rate per month for each patient they see, they have built-in incentives to provide cost-efficient and effective care and avoid overutilization of services. Therefore, the HMO arrangement places risk upon the contracted providers within the HMO to effectively manage the care of enrollees within that capitated pay scale.

5. D: A flexible spending account (FSA), health savings account (HSA), and health reimbursement arrangement (HRA) all help pay medical expenses and are funded, at least in part, with pre-tax dollars. They differ in the kind of insurance plan they work with, who has ownership of them, and who funds them.

6. D: HSAs have been growing steadily in popularity since their introduction in 2003 as part of the Medicare Prescription Drug, Improvement, and Modernization Act. A health savings account (HSA) is a tax advantaged savings/checking account designed for use with a high-deductible health plan (HDHP). Funds in the account are owned by the insured, but the account can be opened by either the individual or by an employer.

7. C: There are three different ways someone can become eligible for Medicare.

- First, when individuals reach 65, they become eligible to enroll in both Medicare Parts A and B.
- Second, if individuals receive either Social Security Disability Insurance (SSDI) or Railroad Retirement Board (RRB) disability benefits, they become eligible for Medicare after 24 months.
- Third, have one of two specific diagnoses. If an individual is not yet 65 but has been diagnosed with either end-stage renal disease (ESRD) or amyotrophic lateral sclerosis (ALS), commonly known as Lou Gehrig's disease, he or she becomes eligible for Medicare. Once an individual is diagnosed with ALS, it is important he or she immediately applies for SSDI to be eligible for Medicare. Once approved, the insured will automatically be enrolled in Medicare the first month he or she receives benefits. There is no waiting period for Medicare for those diagnosed with ALS or ESRD.

8. B: Part D has four phases of coverage.

- The first is the deductible phase in which you pay the full cost of your prescriptions until you reach the deductible. The deductible varies among plans, but no plan may have one higher than $480 in 2022.
- Second is the initial coverage period, in which you pay either a copay or coinsurance amount on each drug up until the limit of $4,430 in 2022.
- When you cross this threshold, you have entered the third phase, or coverage gap, and must pay 25 percent of the cost of each drug. You could pay more in the coverage gap phase if 25 percent of the drugs is higher than the coinsurance or copayment amount you paid in the initial coverage period. The coverage gap, sometimes referred to as the "donut hole," costs used to be higher than 25 percent and enrollees were responsible for 100 percent of drug costs in this phase, but the Affordable Care Act helped enrollees by lowering that amount each year until it reached 25 percent in 2020.
- The fourth phase is the catastrophic coverage phase that you reach when your out-of-pocket costs exceed $7,050 in 2022. In this phase, your copay or coinsurance costs are very low (about 5 percent), and you remain in this phase for the remainder of the plan year.

9. D: Employer-sponsored plans began expanding during World War II because of wage controls imposed on employers by the federal government. The labor market was difficult for employers because of the increased demand for goods and decreased supply of workers while America was at war. The wage and price controls imposed on employers did not allow them to increase wages sufficiently to attract employees. By offering health insurance to prospective employees, employers were able to recruit employees despite not being able to increase their wages. This change was able to occur because the National War Labor Board ruled that fringe benefits, including sick leave and health insurance, did not apply as wages for the purpose of wage controls. As a result, employers began offering improved fringe benefit packages, including health care coverage.

10. A: Fee-for-service plans, also called indemnity plans, are arrangements in which doctors and other health care providers are reimbursed for each individual service they render to insured patients, such as an office visit, laboratory test, or surgical procedure. The allowable amount is the amount that the insurer will pay for each given service, usually based on a negotiated fee schedule that is established with a group of health care providers. Under a fee-for-service plan, the insured is usually required to pay for services upfront and then seek reimbursement from the insurance company. As with other insurance policies, fee-for-service plans require insureds to pay a monthly premium, a deductible, and coinsurance.

11. B: When using a defined contribution health plan, employers give employees a specific dollar amount (a defined contribution) to apply to their benefit costs. Through these coverage plans, the employee, not the employer, manages the allocation of the money provided to meet his or her unique health care needs. The funds provided by the employer by the defined contribution health plan are used by employees to pay for the individual health insurance costs they incur. Compared to traditional group health insurance coverage, these plans can be an affordable alternative for employers. Because these plans do not directly pay for health care provided by medical doctors, hospitals, and the like, they are not considered health insurance plans in the traditional sense.

12. D: The federal Consolidated Omnibus Budget Reconciliation Act of 1985 (COBRA) added health care continuation requirements allowing individuals to keep their health insurance coverage for up to 18 months or longer under certain circumstances. When an individual leaves an employer, under certain circumstances, he or she can choose COBRA continuation to continue the same health coverage. COBRA continuation coverage permits employees and their dependents under a group health plan to continue their coverage if a qualifying event causes them to lose it. Among the qualifying events listed in the statute are:

- Voluntary or forced termination or reduced work hours
- Death of the insured
- Legal separation or divorce that ends an ex-spouse's coverage eligibility
- Loss of dependent child status

There are two circumstances under which an extension of COBRA continuation for up to an additional 18 months (beyond the original 18 months) may become available. This could occur either when the insured confronts a second qualifying event or when a qualified beneficiary is found to be disabled by the Social Security Administration. A second qualifying event could include:

- The death of the covered employee
- The divorce or legal separation of the covered employee and spouse
- The covered employee becoming entitled to Medicare

To get the extension, the qualified beneficiary must notify the plan administrator of an SSA disability determination or of the second qualifying event.

13. C: HIPAA requires covered entities and business associates to comply with certain security and privacy requirements to protect the confidentiality of protected health information (PHI). Covered entity means:

- A health plan
- A health care clearinghouse
- A health care provider who transmits any health information electronically related to transactions regulated by HIPAA

A health plan means individual or group coverage that provides or pays for health care services (e.g., health insurance companies, Medicare, Medicaid, etc.). An employer is not typically a covered entity as defined under the HIPAA law. A health care clearinghouse is an entity that processes health care information. Health care providers include doctors, dentists, and nursing homes, among many others.

14. A: Long-term care insurance covers a range of services and supports individuals to meet their personal care needs and maintain their independence. Most long-term care is not medical care, but rather assistance with the basic personal tasks of everyday living, called activities of daily living (ADLs). ADLs are activities like bathing, dressing, and eating. A long-term care (LTC) insurance policy helps cover the expenses of extended care for people who need help with these activities. The services covered by LTC insurance are not covered by private group or individual health insurance plans or Medicare. Medicaid does provide some long-term care, but not nearly as comprehensively as LTC insurance.

15. B: Under a long-term care insurance policy, the elimination period is the number of days between when the insured starts needing care and when the insured starts receiving payments for the care services. During this time, the insured must pay for his or her care out of pocket. The schedule of benefits page in a long-term care insurance policy states the specific elimination period of the insured's policy. During the elimination period the insured must become chronically ill and receive primary services (other than hospice care and respite care) before certain benefits become payable. Benefits will not be paid for covered services the policyholder receives during this time. No elimination period is required for the insured to receive benefits for hospice care, respite care, needs assessment, or informal caregiver training. The days that count toward the elimination period might or might not be required to be consecutive days.

16. C: As long-term care costs continue to rise much faster than the rate of inflation, insurers have an important rider for consumers to consider purchasing to add value to their policy over the long haul. Many states now require it as an option in insurer's LTC insurance policies. Some insurers include it as part of the policy itself while others offer it as an inflation protection rider.

17. C: The life insurance and long-term care insurance combination product provides a unique benefit package that leverages both life and long-term care insurance. Some individuals consider it a waste to pay long-term care insurance premiums and possibly never need long-term care. The provisions of the Pension Protection Act (PPA) of 2006 provide tax benefits for these long-term care combination plans. These new benefits apply for annuity contracts and life insurance policies. The PPA permits the tax-free distribution of a life insurance or annuity cash value to pay for long-term care. These plans work by tapping the life insurance policy's death benefit and using it to pay for long-term care if needed. The benefit is drawn down to pay for care, and whatever is used reduces the total balance of the life insurance benefit.

18. D: An alternative to traditional long-term care insurance is a qualified state long-term care partnership program. Partnership programs are an innovative cooperative between private insurance carriers and state governments that address the financing of long-term care and reduce pressure on state Medicaid programs. In states with LTC partnership programs in place, the state's Medicaid program eligibility requirements are adjusted so that potential insureds have financial incentives to buy private LTC coverage. The partnership plans work by allowing those with long-term care insurance benefits that have been exhausted under an insurance policy to apply and get benefits through Medicaid. So, if the cost of his or her care exceeds the insurance policy's benefit level, the insured can apply for and receive additional long-term care coverage under Medicaid, thus creating a partnership.

19. A: Critical illness policies typically cover medical emergencies like strokes, heart attacks, organ transplants, cancer, and other life-altering conditions. The purpose of critical illness plans is to help insureds offset the enormous costs of medical care and help replace lost wages after experiencing a medical emergency. If an insured or insured dependent is diagnosed with a covered critical illness, the insurer will typically pay out a lump-sum cash payment to the insured to use in whatever ways he or she chooses. Unlike traditional health insurance, a hospital or physician does not submit claims to the insurer for coverage and reimbursement. The policy's proceeds can be used by the insured to cover payments toward his or her mortgage, medical bills, and living expenses while recuperating. The insured can also apply the benefit funds to experimental medical treatments not covered by his or her health insurance policy.

20. B: Coverage for dental services provided within dental insurance plans is generally categorized into four distinct categories:

- Preventive coverage includes routine cleanings and exams to prevent dental issues and deterioration of teeth.
- Basic services generally include teeth cleanings, x-rays, and cavity fillings.
- Major services typically include more intensive restorative services such as crowns, root canals, and dental surgery to repair and restore damaged teeth.
- Orthodontic coverage includes braces and other appliances to realign or shift teeth to allow better spacing and alignment of teeth.

Health Policy Revisions, Clauses, and Riders

1. A: The entire contract clause states that all pieces of the agreement between insurer and insured are found in the contract. This clause functions primarily for the protection of the insured. It means that the insurance policy, along with the application and any added conditions, represent the entire contract sold to the insured. After the insurance policy documents are issued, the insurer is allowed zero discretion thereafter in making changes to the contract or policy. Once a policy has been issued, the only changes permitted are those proposed and made by the policyholder themselves through endorsements, riders, or amendments. This clause, therefore, keeps the insurance company from making arbitrary changes to the policy provisions when the insured files a claim.

2. C: An exclusionary rider was an amendment that used to be allowed in individual health insurance policies that permanently excluded coverage for a health condition, body part, or body system. With the enactment of the ACA, starting in September 2010, exclusionary riders became prohibited and no longer were able to be applied to coverage for children. Starting in 2014, exclusionary riders became prohibited on any health insurance coverage.

3. B: One standard inclusion required by state law in insurance policies is the notice of claim provision. The notice of claim provision mandates that the insured provide information to the insurance company concerning a covered loss under the policy as soon as possible. Late notice of a covered loss may hamper the ability of the insurance company to complete its review and accurately determine whether the insured is eligible for benefits. Failure by the insured to act in a timely manner to provide notice of a claim could result in the insurance company not being required to make the claims payments.

4. D: The CMS-1500 form is the official Medicare and Medicaid health insurance claim form required by the Centers for Medicare and Medicaid Services (CMS) of the US Department of Health and Human Services. Private health insurance plans use the CMS-1500 form as well. The form was developed by the independent National Uniform Claim Committee (NUCC). The CMS-1500 claim form is also used by all health care-related suppliers that send claims to Medicare-contracted claims administrators, as well as by all non-facility-oriented medical providers (e.g., a doctor's office, as opposed to a facility setting, such as a hospital).

5. D: The insurer receives the claim, evaluates it, and may request more information from the provider if there is any ambiguity regarding the services provided. The insurer then completes the processing of the claim and prepares an explanation of benefits (EOB) for both the insured and the provider. The EOB provides a detailed summary of how the claim was paid, including:

- The date of service (DOS)
- Procedure performed and its diagnostic code
- Provider's charge or billed amount
- Insured's financial responsibility (e.g., copays, deductibles, coinsurance, etc.)
- Final amount paid by the insurer to the provider

6. C: Age is one of the most important factors in how much an insurer decides to charge an individual for coverage. A misstatement of the applicant's age can mean a change of hundreds or more dollars per month in the premium owed. Insurers include a statement in most health and life contracts putting in place the action to be taken if a misstatement of age is discovered after the policy is in force. This is one of the most important provisions for individual health insurance policies. If it is found that the age of the applicant was accidentally misstated, the insurer can adjust premium payments and policy benefits. An insurer may decide to terminate insurance coverage of an individual who intentionally misstates his or her age on a life or health insurance application.

7. D: Coinsurance is the percentage of the billed amount that the insured is responsible for paying after the insured has already met his or her deductible. Typically, the higher the percentage of coinsurance for which an insured is responsible, the less expensive the monthly insurance premium is. To avoid the possibility of a catastrophic medical cost causing severe financial hardship for an insured, insurers apply a cap on the total medical costs an insured will pay in a year, which includes coinsurance, deductible amounts, and copays. This cap is called the annual out-of-pocket maximum. When the out-of-pocket maximum for the plan year has been reached, the insurer pays 100 percent of covered, eligible charges for the remainder of the plan year.

8. B: The term usual, reasonable, and customary (UCR) is the amount paid for a medical claim in a geographic area based on what similar providers in the same area typically charge for the same or equivalent medical treatment. Insurance companies use UCR information to determine what reimbursement rate they should set for that specific service item in that geographic area. Often the UCR amount is used by insurance companies to set fee schedules when insureds see out-of-network providers for their health care needs.

9. A: Noncancellable insurance policies are not exactly the same as guaranteed renewable policies, because the latter only ensure that the insurer has to continue coverage as long as the insured pays his or her premiums. They do not ensure that the premiums stay at the same rate. Some guaranteed renewable policies may increase in premium, while noncancellable policies will not.

10. B: Double indemnity is a life insurance clause or provision in which the company agrees to pay double the policy's stated benefit amount in the case of an accidental death. Insurance companies can also offer triple indemnity. If this option is available, beneficiaries may receive three times the face amount of the policy if an accident is the insured's cause of death. Many insurance companies define the type of accidents that qualifies for the AD&D rider. Accidents are unexpected happenings, such as car accidents and plane crashes. Although double and triple indemnity clauses cover accidental deaths, these causes of death are excluded:

- Suicide
- Murder or conspiracy by any beneficiaries of the policy
- Death caused by the insured's own gross negligence
- Death by natural causes, like heart disease and cancer

Social Insurance

1. C: Medicare Advantage (MA) Plans, also called Medicare Part C, are private health plans for Medicare participants. The private insurance companies that offer Medicare Part C plans are contracted by the federal government to provide Medicare benefits, essentially taking the place of Original Medicare. As stipulated by their federal contracts, Medicare Advantage Plans are usually required to cover at least the same amount of health care services as Original Medicare. Some of these plans provide additional coverage beyond what's included with Original Medicare. Those extra benefits often include:

- Prescription drug coverage
- Vision
- Dental
- Hearing benefits

Under a Medical Advantage Plan, some services may not be covered in all facilities or provider settings.

2. A: Medicare supplement insurance plans, also called Medigap, help pay for some of the out-of-pocket costs that Original Medicare doesn't cover. Medicare supplement plans are offered by private insurance companies and help provide additional coverage to the coverage already provided through Medicare Parts A and B. For instance, enrollment in Medicare Part B provides coverage for 80 percent of physician charges. If an individual purchases a Medicare supplement plan, it generally complements Original Medicare so that the two combined provide complete coverage; the supplemental plan pays the remaining 20 percent of health care charges if the provider accepts Medicare assignment. A provider that does not accept Medicare assignment can charge up to 15 percent beyond Medicare's cost assignment. For Medicare Part A, supplement policies cover the Medicare Part A deductibles and coinsurance to effectively cover most, if not all, related expenses with the combination. Of course, Medicare participants that purchase a Medicare supplement must pay the Medicare premium out-of-pocket.

3. B: To receive Medicare Part D (prescription drug coverage), enrollees must sign up with a plan managed by a private insurer. Individuals have options and can choose either a prescription drug plan (PDP) or a Medicare Advantage Plan. A PDP plan adds Medicare Part D benefits to Original Medicare coverage. Unlike Medicare supplement plan premiums, the cost of Medicare Part D benefits is largely based on the enrollee's income. If income exceeds a benchmark, then that individual may pay more than a senior with a lower income.

4. D: Coordination of benefits (COB) is a term used when an insured is enrolled in two or more health insurance plans. The two insurers share information and coordinate benefits to make sure extra dollars are not unknowingly paid for the insured's medical care. The insurance industry has developed rules to determine which plan pays primary, secondary, and tertiary. For example, if both spouses are employees on their respective insurance plans, their primary coverage is through their employer, and the secondary coverage is then through the spouse's employer.

5. C: The Social Security (SS) and Supplemental Security Income (SSI) disability programs provide disability benefits and services to millions of disabled Americans. These two programs have similarities:

- Both are administered by the Social Security Administration.
- Both provide needed benefits (specifically income) that aid vulnerable populations.
- To gain access to benefits under each program, the individual must have a disability and medically determinable impairments.

SSI is a federal income supplement program funded by general tax revenues (not Social Security taxes). Its purpose is to aid aged, blind, and disabled persons who have little or no income regardless of work history or Social Security payments.

Other Health Insurance Concepts

1. B: An individual is considered partially disabled if the disability prevents him or her from performing one or more, but not all, primary tasks of his or her work, limits the amount of time or specified number of hours the individual is able to work, or causes his or her income to be reduced. With a partial disability benefit, the individual is also compensated for the time lost on the job. Residual disability benefits, comparatively, are based on a reduction or loss of an individual's earning power. Under this scenario, the disability income insurance benefit is graduated and equal to the earning power the insured has lost. If the individual's income loss is 70 percent because of the disability, the individual will receive 70 percent of the total disability benefit while he or she remains disabled. Certain restrictions may apply to different policies in terms of maximum benefit payout or capped percentage losses.

2. A: The coordination of benefits clause is now a uniform provision for virtually all health insurance policies. This provision determines how duplicate coverage is administered when an insured or dependent has coverage under two different policies.

- The primary plan will pay its full, normal benefits—no more, no less. The primary plan is ordinarily the one in which the insured is the employee, and the secondary plan is usually the one where the insured is a dependent.
- The secondary plan will normally pay what is remaining of the total medical bill for services it allows under the policy, up to the maximum amount it would have paid if it were the sole insurance company for the patient.

3. C: Managed care is a health care delivery method that seeks to control the costs of health care services while improving health care quality. Managed care organizations typically contract with a group of selected providers and discourage access to providers outside of that group. To encourage the use of contracted providers, the managed care organization provides fewer benefits for services from noncontracted providers. Managed care organizations include:

- Health maintenance organizations (HMO)
- Preferred provider organizations (PPO)
- Point-of-service plans (POS)

4. B: Case management is the means used by health insurers to improve the coordination of services on behalf of an individual person with a severe illness or chronic health condition when there are many different health care providers treating the individual. Case management for health insurance companies is typically performed by health care professionals with nursing experience to assure expert involvement. By managing medical care more closely, case managers ensure that health care services are efficient, effective, and appropriate for each individual's health and circumstances.

5. D: Subrogation is the process used by insurers to investigate and determine if a third party is responsible for the health care coverage of an injury caused to one of their policyholders. If the insurer's investigation reveals the other party is responsible for the claim, the insurance carrier has the legal right to seek reimbursement from the responsible party. Subrogation comes into play often between health insurance and auto insurance. For instance, an insured of XYZ Insurance goes to the emergency room with a broken ankle. The insurance company receives no notice that the injury was sustained in an auto accident. Two months later, XYZ insurance learns that the insured's car was hit by another driver and this resulted in the broken ankle. XYZ insurance begins the subrogation process of reaching out to the other driver's auto insurance provider for reimbursement of the policy benefits paid under the insured's health insurance plan.

Field Underwriting Procedures

1. A: It is important to understand the differences between an insurance broker and an insurance agent. An insurance agent usually represents one specific insurance carrier. The positives of working with an insurance agent can be a lower rate, easier plan changes, and a closer working relationship with the insurer. Meanwhile, an insurance broker works with multiple insurance carriers. The positive of working with a broker is a broker will provide the applicant with various policy options at different rates. The broker can offer a customer more coverage options than an insurance agent since the latter is usually limited to one carrier. Salaries for agents and brokers are largely based on commissions, so keeping clients happy and renewing their coverage is beneficial for both.

2. C: The Fair Credit Reporting Act (FCRA) requires that an applicant be told if a consumer report is requested and be informed of the details of the possible investigation. It protects policyholder's privacy rights and helps to ensure that credit report information is valid when presented and available in credit reports. The FCRA seeks to promote the accuracy, fairness, and privacy of a patient's information. If a health insurer declines the application because of information learned from the applicant's credit report, the insurer is required to provide the applicant the name and address of the reporting agency they used.

3. C: MIB Group, Inc. (formerly the Medical Information Bureau) is an interchange of health information insurers refer to during the underwriting process. Insurance companies use MIB reports to assess insurance applicants and the risks they represent, catching errors, misstatements, and oversights offered within an individual's insurance application. Companies submit underwriting information to MIB, and that information can then be accessed by other underwriters. The information is coded and used exclusively by the insurance companies that are members. An individual's MIB record includes the medical status and conditions that might impact an individual's long-term health outlook. An MIB report includes the following type of information:

- Medical impairments or conditions
- When the medical condition was treated and/or diagnosed
- The types of treatments the applicant received
- The source of the medical history
- The date of any previous life insurance applications

MIB gathers and obtains the materials presented with the applicant's consent. Insurance companies must use MIB information as a signal of potential discrepancies only; the information cannot be used as a stand-alone definitive source and must be verified through a secondary resource.

4. D: A life insurance policy is not the type of contract that is negotiated between equal parties. Instead, the contract is drafted by one party (the insurer) with no input or discussion from the other party (policyholder). The policyholder must either accept or reject the contract as is. The policyholder does not have the option of negotiating, revising, or deleting any of the document's content. This type of contract is called an adhesion contract. Due to the nature of this type of contract, courts generally interpret any ambiguity existing in an insurance contract in the policyholder's favor because of that unequal relationship. Courts have regularly ruled in the policyholder's favor by allowing reasonable expectations on the part of the policyholder (or the named beneficiaries), because the contract is prepared solely by the insurer without input from the policyholder.

5. B: The certificate of insurance is a document issued by an insurance company that serves as proof that the insurance coverage and its specific coverage provisions exists. Among the items included in the certificate of insurance are:

- The effective date of coverage
- The policy type purchased by the insured
- The policy's coverage terms, limitations, and exclusions

A certificate of insurance is often requested by attorneys during litigation where parties are disputing liability and coverage specifics. If, for example, coverage for a specific medical procedure is up for debate, a certificate of insurance may be requested to verify and determine whether the surgery is a covered benefit, limitation, or exclusion to the policy.

6. B: A material representation is a statement that gets someone to agree to a contract that the party would not have agreed to without that statement being made. An example might be if an applicant failed to mention that they have a chronic disease for which they simply decided not to take medicine. If the insurer knew the applicant had a chronic disease that may cause future health problems, the insurer may have decided not to issue the policy, or issue it with different policy terms or a higher premium. This might be considered a material misrepresentation worthy of voiding the contract.

Practice Test

Want to take this practice test in an online interactive format?
Check out the bonus page, which includes interactive practice questions and
much more: **mometrix.com/bonus948/lifehealth**

1. What would be the best course of action for an individual with a $10,000 life insurance policy if they want to maintain their life insurance coverage while still being able to qualify for Medicaid?

    a. Cash out the whole life policy and purchase a term policy.
    b. Take out a loan on the policy.
    c. Sell the policy.
    d. Transfer the policy ownership to their spouse.

2. Who is allowed to make changes to the wording of a life insurance contract?

    a. Nobody
    b. An executive officer of the insurance company
    c. An insurance agent
    d. The policyholder

3. Robert applied for a life insurance policy and paid the initial premium. Robert died in a car accident before the policy could be issued. The insurance company discovered that Robert was treated for angina the year before and would've denied Robert's application had he not died. The insurance company denied the claim to pay the death benefit even though Robert did not die of angina based on which of the following?

    a. The insurer has no obligation to pay an insurance contract until the policy is delivered.
    b. The conditional receipt that Robert was issued upon completing the application
    c. The fact that Robert forgot to mention that he was treated briefly for angina
    d. The material misrepresentation Robert made during the application

4. Which type of policy offers the policyholder a flexible premium payment?

    a. Term
    b. Whole life
    c. Variable life
    d. Universal life

5. Which of the following describes how Medicaid is administered?

    a. At the federal government level
    b. At the state government level
    c. Under contract by private insurers
    d. By Medicare

6. Which of the following types of disability is defined as the inability to perform one or more duties of one's occupation?

  a. Partial
  b. Recurrent
  c. Residual
  d. Total

7. Which of the following is NOT a requirement for a health insurance company if it cancels an individual's policy?

  a. Send the insured at least a 90-day notice
  b. Provide notice to the state
  c. Treat all insureds the same, regardless of health
  d. Offer a replacement plan if available

8. In a traditional whole life policy, what amount is the insurer at risk to pay in the event of the insured's death?

  a. Face value plus the cash value
  b. Face value minus any partial surrender
  c. Face value minus the cash value
  d. Face value minus separate account value

9. Which of the following most accurately describes a payor benefit?

  a. Pays the premium if the policyowner dies or becomes disabled
  b. Provides level term coverage for the policyowner
  c. Allows the policyowner to increase the death benefit without evidence of insurability
  d. Provides for interest-free loans to the policyowner

10. Which set of regulations governs the handling of sensitive and private medical information provided during the policy application process?

  a. FCRA
  b. HIPAA
  c. ERISA
  d. MIB

11. A living needs rider can be added to every policy type EXCEPT:

  a. Universal life
  b. 10-year term
  c. Variable universal life
  d. Whole life

12. All of the following are NOT typically covered under a vision insurance plan EXCEPT:

  a. Contact lenses
  b. Safety glasses
  c. Lost or broken lenses or frames
  d. Eye injuries

13. Which of the following is NOT a feature of a group life insurance policy?

    a. Can be written to 2x or 3x the employee's annual salary

    b. Can provide coverage for the spouse and children of the employee

    c. Option to convert to a whole life policy upon retirement

    d. Builds cash value payable upon retirement

14. An insured falls off a ladder and injures his ankle while stocking items at work on Friday, March 10. He goes to the doctor the next day, who advises him that it is broken and not to return to work for the next 30 days. He informs his HR department of the injury the following Monday, March 13, along with the doctor's report. If his short-term disability policy at work has a 14-day elimination period, at what date can he expect the STD policy benefits to begin?

    a. March 10

    b. March 13

    c. March 24

    d. March 27

15. Robert has already paid his annual $3,000 health insurance deductible during the first 10 months of the year. He has additional medical expenses in November totaling $1,200. How will this expense affect his deductible for next year if his health plan has a carryover provision?

    a. Robert would pay $900 in November and the remaining $300 the following year.

    b. The $1,200 Robert paid in November would apply toward next year's deductible.

    c. His deductible would reset to $3,000 the following January.

    d. Robert would pay $600 in November and the remaining $600 the following year.

16. Which of the following is NOT considered by an insurer when underwriting a group health policy?

    a. Group policy claims history

    b. Overall group health history

    c. Personnel turnover history

    d. Group industry classification

17. How long does an insurer have to reject an application for a lapsed policy reinstatement?

    a. 30 days

    b. 45 days

    c. 60 days

    d. 90 days

18. All of the following are advantages of an indexed annuity EXCEPT:

    a. They are insured by the FDIC.

    b. They can be structured to provide lifetime income.

    c. Money grows tax-deferred.

    d. They do not lose money during market downturns.

19. Which of the following is considered the primary purpose of an elimination period for disability insurance plans?

    a. To reduce the cost of a policy

    b. To prevent fraudulent claims

    c. To provide the insurer an opportunity to investigate the validity of a claim

    d. To give the provider ample time to process the claim

20. Janet is applying for a life insurance policy but has diabetes. What tool would an insurance company NOT rely on in order to accurately assess Janet's insurability?

    a. A sworn statement from Janet's attorney

    b. Observations made by the agent

    c. Credit reports

    d. A statement from Janet's physician

21. Paul is attempting to purchase a health plan from a private insurer. He completed an application on May 13, and the policy was put into effect on May 25. According to the 30-day policy probationary period, on what date is Paul eligible to file a claim on his policy?

    a. May 13

    b. May 25

    c. June 13

    d. June 25

22. Which of the following regarding a long-term care rider is FALSE?

    a. Provides long-term care benefits in addition to the policy death benefit

    b. Benefits are paid income tax-free.

    c. Requires evidence of inability to perform daily tasks

    d. Provides up to 100 percent of policy benefits if the insured qualifies

23. How does an insurer treat the misstatement of age in a life insurance policy after the two-year contestability period?

    a. The insurer would pay the adjusted premium from the policy's cash value.

    b. The insurer would cancel the policy.

    c. The policy face amount would be adjusted to pay what the premiums would purchase for the corrected age.

    d. The insurer would require back premiums to pay the premium difference.

24. Which of the following death benefit settlement options is tax-free?

    a. Fixed amount

    b. Interest only

    c. Lump sum

    d. Lifetime income

25. Which type of policy does NOT utilize a general account by the insurer?

    a. Universal life

    b. Variable universal life

    c. Term insurance

    d. Variable life

26. All of the following are features and benefits of Medicare Supplement plans EXCEPT:

    a. Requires both Medicare Part A and Part B coverage
    b. Can provide coverage outside of the US
    c. Is guaranteed renewable
    d. Includes prescription drug coverage

27. Helen will be turning 65 next month. She is being offered a Medicare plan that will pay her monthly premiums for signing up. What type of Medicare plan is Helen being offered?

    a. Medicare Part A
    b. Medicare Part B
    c. Medicare Part C
    d. Medicare Part D

28. Which of the following definitions of a disability usually requires the highest premium for a disability income policy?

    a. Own Occupation
    b. Any Occupation
    c. Total Disability
    d. Permanent Disability

29. All of the following should be considered when determining whether a policy is a replacement to an existing policy EXCEPT:

    a. Does the insured have other insurance policies?
    b. Does the insured have any other pending applications with another insurer?
    c. Has the insured recently taken out loan(s) against any other policies?
    d. Has the insured canceled life insurance in the past?

30. Which of the following could potentially reduce the face amount of a universal life policy?

    a. Partial withdrawal
    b. Late payment of premium
    c. Policy loan
    d. Decreasing term rider

31. What is the primary purpose of the spendthrift clause of a life insurance policy?

    a. Protects the death benefit against creditors of the insured or beneficiary
    b. Prevents the beneficiary from electing their own settlement options
    c. Protects the ownership of the policy against creditors
    d. Protects against policy reassignment

32. An individual purchases a life insurance policy that was issued on March 1, 2010. The insured failed to disclose a finding of high cholesterol discovered in 2009. Which of the following options fully describes the time period during which the insurance company would be required to pay the claim if the insured dies of a heart attack?

    a. Any time after the policy was issued
    b. Any time after 6 months has elapsed since the policy was issued
    c. Any time after 1 year has elapsed since the policy was issued
    d. Any time after 2 years has elapsed since the policy was issued

33. Which of the following types of insurance policies represents an indexed life policy?

    a. Term life
    b. Whole life
    c. Universal life
    d. Variable life

34. Kathy is currently enrolled in a Medicare Advantage plan. She is also covered under her husband's health care plan at work that covers all five employees. If Kathy requires a hip replacement surgery, which insurance plan would cover the surgery?

    a. Both plans would cover her equally.
    b. Her Medicare Advantage plan would cover 60 percent of the cost.
    c. Her husband's insurance plan would cover most of the cost.
    d. Her Medicare Advantage plan would cover most of the cost.

35. A homeowner attempting to fix a leak on his roof falls and dies three years after purchasing life insurance. The insurance company denies the claim, stating that a clause in the insurance contract specifically prohibits the insured's "engaging in any inherently dangerous activities." If the beneficiary sues the insurance company, what would be the most likely outcome?

    a. The insurer would be forced to pay, since it never defined what constituted a dangerous activity.
    b. The insurer would not be forced to pay, since climbing on a wet roof is considered a dangerous activity.
    c. The insurer would not be forced to pay but would be required to return all premiums paid.
    d. The insurer would not be forced to pay, since the accident occurred after the two-year contestability period of the policy.

36. Which of the following would NOT be considered an aleatory contract?

    a. Boat insurance
    b. Life insurance
    c. A home improvement loan
    d. A lottery ticket

37. Which of the following would NOT be a reason to obtain short-term medical insurance?

    a. To obtain coverage while in-between jobs
    b. To obtain coverage after missing the deadline for open enrollment
    c. If unable to afford the premiums of a major medical plan
    d. To increase the insurance coverage of a major medical plan

38. Which of the following regarding key person insurance policies is FALSE?

    a. Premiums are tax-deductible for the business.
    b. Pays for loss of revenue due to the key person's disability
    c. Pays for the hiring and training of a replacement employee while key employee is disabled
    d. Provides for tax-free payments for the business

39. Which policy option is designed to circumvent probate court upon the death of the insured?

    a. The nonforfeiture clause
    b. The policyowner
    c. The absolute assignment
    d. The named beneficiary

40. What does the back-end load of a deferred annuity contract refer to?

    a. Nonforfeiture provision
    b. Settlement options
    c. Tax deferment
    d. Surrender charges

41. All of the following are elements of an insurable risk EXCEPT:

    a. Risk of loss must be unpredictable.
    b. Loss must be due to chance only.
    c. Loss must be unexpected.
    d. Loss exposures must be randomly selected.

42. All of the following accurately describe workers' compensation insurance EXCEPT:

    a. Administered by the federal government
    b. Provides medical and wage benefits for people injured at work
    c. Protects businesses from civil suits from those injured on the job
    d. Pays death benefits to families of those killed on the job

43. When delivering an insurance policy to an insured, which of the following items might an insurance agent review with an insured that was not reviewed at the time of the application?

    a. Policy provisions
    b. Riders
    c. Ratings
    d. Exclusions

44. At what time is a policyowner required to demonstrate an insurable interest in the life of the insured?

    a. At the time of death of the insured
    b. At the time the policy endows
    c. After the two-year contestability period
    d. At the time the policy is written

45. What is the purpose of the 7-pay test regarding modified endowment contracts?

    a. It ensures that life insurance contracts are not used as tax shelters.
    b. It ensures that enough money is paid into the contract to cover the monthly cost of insurance.
    c. It ensures that the policy is set to endow at age 100.
    d. It ensures that the policy has enough cash value to fund long-term care.

46. Which of the following is considered a provision of a policy loan?

a. Policy loans are interest-free.
b. Policy loans are subtracted from the policy's cash value.
c. Policy loans not paid back are subtracted from the policy's face amount.
d. Policy loans are available once the policy has been in effect for one year.

47. What is the purpose of a nonforfeiture option in an insurance contract?

a. To guarantee the policy value in the event of lapse
b. To provide for policy reassignment
c. To guarantee the death benefit
d. To guarantee the rate of return

48. Which of the following best describes usual, reasonable, and customary (URC) charges?

a. Pre-negotiated fees between an insurer and providers
b. Average fee charged by providers in a given area
c. Fees charged according to the schedule set by the American Medical Association
d. Fees charged according to age

49. Which of the following would NOT be a reason to consider a life settlement for a life insurance policy?

a. When an insured wants to reduce their tax liability
b. When an insured can no longer afford the policy premiums
c. When an insured needs money for an emergency
d. When the insured no longer needs the policy

50. Fred worked in sales at the cable company before taking a job as an installer, but he never informed his private health insurer of the change in occupation. He was recently injured when falling from the bucket on the lift truck. How did the insurance company handle the claim?

a. The insurer denied coverage.
b. The insurer only paid the claim up to the amount that his original premium would have covered.
c. The insurer paid the claim in full but charged Fred the back premium difference that his new job requires.
d. The insurer paid the claim in full and canceled the policy.

51. Which of the following is NOT part of the insuring clause of an insurance contract?

a. The insurer's promise to pay
b. The parties of the contract
c. Requirement for proof of loss
d. Frequency and amount of premium

52. In what scenario would a policyowner normally create an irrevocable beneficiary?

a. A court order
b. A bankruptcy
c. A policy for a juvenile
d. An insured on Medicare

53. Ray is a 63-year-old who enjoys sailing. He wants to obtain life insurance in the event that something should happen while out on the water but is worried about the cost. What type of policy should Ray consider?

   a. A universal life policy
   b. A term policy
   c. An accidental death and dismemberment policy
   d. A whole life policy

54. The free look period of an insurance policy is usually how many days?

   a. 30 days
   b. 10 days
   c. 60 days
   d. 3 days

55. All of the following are types of policy maximum benefit limits EXCEPT:

   a. Lifetime policy limit
   b. Annual policy limit
   c. Monthly policy limit
   d. Per-cause policy limit

56. What tool do insurers use to determine an insured's medical history?

   a. FCRA report
   b. MIB report
   c. AMA report
   d. CLUE report

57. John and his wife each had an insurance policy, naming each other as the primary beneficiary and their respective parents as the secondary beneficiaries. If both insureds die in a plane crash, how would each insurer determine the order of death and how to pay the death benefit?

   a. Each insurer would determine that their insured died last. The policies would be paid to the estate of their respective insureds.
   b. Each insurer would determine that their insured died last. The policies would be paid to their respective secondary beneficiaries.
   c. Each insurer would determine that their insured died first. The policies would be paid to the estate of their respective insureds.
   d. Each insurer would determine that their insured died first. The policies would be paid to the estate of their respective primary beneficiaries.

58. Which one of the following is NOT considered a typical life insurance policy exclusion?

   a. Piloting an aircraft
   b. Death as a result of war
   c. Traveling to a politically unstable country or region
   d. Suicide

59. Which of these policies does NOT offer a guaranteed minimum death benefit?

a. Variable universal life
b. 20-year term
c. Variable life
d. Indexed universal life

60. All of the following are required by an agent when delivering a policy EXCEPT:

a. Delivery receipt
b. Policy premium
c. Verification that the insured's medical condition has not changed
d. Review of policy representations

61. An insured who is terminally ill is considering his best options regarding his life insurance policy. He needs funds to pay for current expenses. His policy has a living needs rider.

Policy face amount:	$100,000
Cash surrender value:	$64,000
Viatical settlement offer:	$77,000

Which option should the insured consider if he wants to receive the highest amount of benefit for current expenses?

a. Cash out the policy.
b. Accept the viatical settlement offer.
c. Take out a loan on the policy.
d. Activate the living needs benefit on the policy.

62. Which rider will NOT affect the death benefit amount when added to a policy?

a. Guaranteed insurability
b. Accidental death and dismemberment
c. Disability income rider
d. Return of premium

63. Which of the following events concerning a life insurance policy is NOT considered taxable by the IRS?

a. Absolute reassignment of the policy
b. Surrendering the policy for cash value
c. Receiving the death benefit upon the death of the insured
d. The policy becoming a modified endowment contract

64. Which of the following would be considered a material misrepresentation on behalf of the insured?

a. Not revealing a broken leg
b. Not revealing a previous cancer diagnosis
c. Not revealing a previous COVID-19 diagnosis
d. Not revealing a previous DUI conviction

65. A traveling salesperson that is selecting a health care plan during their annual enrollment period is looking for the freedom to choose their own doctors anywhere in the United States. Which of the following health plans should they NOT consider?

    a. A standard major medical plan
    b. POS plan
    c. PPO plan
    d. HMO plan

66. In which of the following situations might it be in the best interest of an insured to replace their existing life insurance policy?

    a. Taking a loan against a whole life policy to purchase another whole life policy
    b. Replacing a term policy with another term policy
    c. Replacing a whole life policy with another whole life policy
    d. Replacing a term policy with a variable universal life policy

67. Which policy option ensures that the premium payments are kept up-to-date?

    a. Paid-up additions
    b. Automatic premium loan
    c. Premium deduction dividend
    d. Waiver of premium

68. What type of policy provides coverage for a business to pay expenses if the owner becomes disabled?

    a. Group disability policy
    b. Business continuation insurance
    c. Business overhead expense policy
    d. Disability buyout

69. An insured has a typical 80/20 major medical insurance plan with a $500 yearly deductible. How much would the insured be required to pay for a $2,000 MRI bill, provided that they had no other claims in the current year?

    a. $400
    b. $500
    c. $800
    d. $900

70. Which of the following pieces of legislation prevents health insurers from excluding preexisting conditions from coverage?

    a. Health Insurance Portability and Accountability Act (HIPAA)
    b. Employee Retirement Income Security Act (ERISA)
    c. Consolidated Omnibus Budget Reconciliation Act (COBRA)
    d. Affordable Care Act (ACA)

71. What is the minimum grace period for a life insurance policy paid monthly?

    a. 3 days
    b. 7 days
    c. 10 days
    d. 31days

72. All of the following can be considered reasons for the purchase of a long-term care (LTC) policy EXCEPT:

    a. Policies are guaranteed renewable.
    b. Benefits are tax-free.
    c. Premiums are tax-deductible.
    d. Provides protection for assets

73. A person has a typical 80/20 high deductible insurance plan with the following:

    $3,000 deductible
    $6,500 maximum out-of-pocket limit

If the yearly medical expenses totaled $19,000, what amount did the insurance company pay?

    a. $12,200
    b. $12,500
    c. $12,800
    d. $16,000

74. All of the following are features of a qualified retirement plan EXCEPT:

    a. They allow for tax-free withdrawals.
    b. They must have a vesting schedule for employer contributions.
    c. They must offer equal benefits to all participating employees.
    d. All eligible employees must be allowed to participate.

75. Which section of an insurance application constitutes the agent's report?

    a. Part I
    b. Part II
    c. Part III
    d. Part IV

76. Janet has a whole life policy with a cash value of $2,800. She takes out a loan on the policy for $800. At what point would Janet be required to pay tax on the policy loan?

    a. Upon receiving the loan
    b. As the loan is paid back
    c. If the policy is surrendered
    d. If the loan is not paid back

77. Which of the following premium payment options represents the lowest cost over the lifetime of a life insurance policy?

    a. Indeterminate premium
    b. Single premium
    c. Modified premium
    d. Monthly premium

78. Which of the following have rights in an insurance policy?

    a. Policyowner, insured, and beneficiary
    b. Policyowner and insured
    c. Policyowner and beneficiary
    d. Policyowner

79. **Which of the following is NOT a feature of a renewable and convertible term policy?**
    a. Insured can renew the term on the renewal date without evidence of insurability.
    b. Insured can convert term to whole life without evidence of insurability.
    c. Insured can renew the term on the renewal date based upon attained age.
    d. Insured can convert term to a whole life policy based upon existing premiums.

80. **An insured with a typical cancer policy with a $1,000 deductible receives cancer treatment, outlining the following expenses:**
    Surgical expenses: $22,000
    Prescription drugs: $13,000
    Outpatient treatment: $2,900
    X-Rays: $1,600

How much would the insurance company be expected to pay under the cancer policy?
    a. $27,500
    b. $35,600
    c. $36,500
    d. $36,900

81. **The consideration clause in an insurance policy contract provides for which of the following?**
    a. List of policy exclusions
    b. The truthfulness of information provided by the insured
    c. The amount of premium and payment schedule in exchange for coverage
    d. Outlines the rights of the policyowner

82. **Which of the following describes a type of contract such as insurance where one side is obligated to perform in exchange for money?**
    a. Bilateral
    b. Adhesion
    c. Aleatory
    d. Unilateral

83. **All of the following can be used by an insurance company when underwriting a policy to deny an application EXCEPT:**
    a. Driving history
    b. Credit history
    c. Race
    d. Medical history

84. **Which of the following is NOT considered a life insurance settlement option?**
    a. Fixed period
    b. Reassignment
    c. Life income option
    d. Interest only

85. Which of the following riders will enable the cash value of a whole life policy to continue as if premiums have been paid?

    a. Guaranteed insurability
    b. Cost of living
    c. Return of cash value
    d. Waiver of premium

86. An insured completed an application for life insurance, which included an additional accidental death benefit, and paid the initial policy premium. If the insured was in excellent health and had no adverse medical history but died of an accident before the policy was issued, what would the insurance company most likely have done since the policy had not yet been issued?

    a. Deny the insurance claim
    b. Pay the accidental death benefit only
    c. Pay the death benefit and the accidental death benefit
    d. Cancel the insurance application and return the premium

87. Which of the following includes the provision that an insured's disability income cannot exceed their actual wage before this disability?

    a. The consideration clause
    b. The insuring clause
    c. Relation of earnings to insurance clause
    d. The entire contract clause

88. Which of the following types of policies would be most appropriate for a person interested in using life insurance to protect their mortgage?

    a. 30-year term
    b. Credit life
    c. Universal life
    d. Annual renewable term

89. Which of the following modes of premium payment represents the greatest cost to the policyholder?

    a. Weekly
    b. Monthly
    c. Semi-annual
    d. Annual

90. Alex mistakenly selected her gender as male instead of female when completing her online life insurance application. The policy was issued without anyone catching the mistake. What would be the insurance company's most likely course of action upon Alex's death?

    a. It would decrease the face amount that the lower premium would've originally purchased.
    b. It would deny coverage as a material misrepresentation.
    c. It would refund the premium difference that rating her as male produced.
    d. It would increase the face amount that the higher premium would've offered.

91. An insurance agent is reviewing the projected investment returns based on historical data that an insured could potentially receive as part of the investments in a variable universal life policy. These statements made by the insurance agent are defined as:

    a. Projections
    b. Expectations
    c. Representations
    d. Warranties

92. Which type of death benefit option provides insurance coverage to two or more persons, payable upon the last insured to die?

    a. Joint life
    b. Joint ownership
    c. Joint survivorship
    d. Joint insured

93. A non-married employee that has elected to contribute the maximum to her health savings account each year had a balance of $12,500 at the end of 2021. If she again contributes the maximum allowed yearly amount for 2022, what will her account balance be at the end of the year if she does not make any withdrawals?

    a. $16,100
    b. $16,150
    c. $19,700
    d. $19,800

94. Which policy dividend option should a policyowner select if their goal is to accrue as much cash value as possible?

    a. Cash
    b. Premium reduction
    c. Paid-up additions
    d. Accumulate at interest

95. How long must an insured wait until legal action can be brought against an insurer?

    a. 30 days
    b. 60 days
    c. 180 days
    d. One year

96. Which of the following would NOT have to be considered when replacing a life insurance policy written by another insurer?

    a. Obtaining the consent of the insured
    b. Providing a Notice of Replacement to the existing policyholder and insurer
    c. Potentially increasing the cost of insurance
    d. Restarting the two-year contestability period

97. A recently terminated employee was informed they have until September 15 to elect for COBRA coverage. What day was the employee likely terminated?

   a. August 15
   b. July 15
   c. June 15
   d. March 15

98. How does Social Security measure a person's eligibility for retirement benefits?

   a. Adjusted gross income
   b. Minimum age of 62
   c. Average amount paid into Social Security through paycheck deductions
   d. Earned credits

99. Which of the following is NOT a feature of a universal life policy?

   a. Guaranteed death benefit
   b. Adjustable face amount
   c. Flexible premiums
   d. Choice of investment options

100. Which of the following provisions of a child rider is FALSE?

   a. Provides level term coverage
   b. Can provide coverage for one or more children
   c. Allows for conversion to a whole life policy without evidence of insurability
   d. Provides coverage for newborns immediately upon birth

Answer Key and Explanations

1. D: Under Medicaid's Community Spouse Resource Allowance, an insured would most likely be able to transfer the ownership of their policy to their spouse. By doing this, the policy would no longer affect their eligibility for Medicaid. Most states only have a $1,500 exemption limit on whole life insurance for insureds in order to qualify for Medicaid. Selling a policy, taking out a loan on a policy, or cashing out a policy would all create assets that would count against the insured's Medicaid eligibility limits.

2. B: Only an executive officer of a life insurance company can permit a change to the wording of a life insurance contract. Any modifications must be in writing as part of the contract and be approved by the policyowner. Insurance agents do not have the authority to introduce modifications to the wording of a policy contract.

3. B: Robert was issued a conditional receipt upon completing the insurance application and paying the initial premium. The conditional receipt is contingent upon an insured's medical condition at the time of the application as well as underwriting approval of the application. Some states would require the insurer in this case to prove that Robert's omission of his previous treatment for angina was intentional before it would allow the insurer to deny a life insurance claim for a policy that it had issued. This would not apply since the policy had not yet been issued. If Robert was in very good health and the insurance company would have approved his application, it would have paid the death benefit under the terms of the conditional receipt even though the policy was not yet delivered.

4. D: Universal life policies offer the policyowner the option of flexible premium payments. Only a suggested target premium is set by the insurer. Variable life, whole life, and term policies have a general account that requires a set, level premium for the cost of insurance.

5. B: Medicaid is a government-sponsored health care program for low-income families and individuals. It is administered at the state government level and paid for primarily by funds provided by the federal government. If a state mandates additional services not provided by the federal government, it must fund these services at the state level.

6. C: Residual disability is defined as the inability to perform one or more duties of a person's occupation. Benefits paid under residual disability are based on a percentage of lost income. Residual disability benefits are typically referred to as "at-work" benefits if the insured is able to work while receiving benefits.

7. B: Health insurance companies are permitted to cancel or non-renew health insurance policies in certain situations. For instance, a health insurer may cancel a policy if the company no longer provides a certain type of policy or no longer offers health insurance. Although an insurer is not required to notify any particular state if it cancels a policy, it must provide a 90-day notice of cancellation, it cannot cancel a policy based on an insured's health, and it must offer an insured a suitable replacement policy if it has one available that it offers to others.

8. C: A traditional whole life policy is designed to endow when the insured reaches the age of 100, when the cash value of the policy matches the death benefit. Since the cash value of a whole life policy does not increase the face amount, the insurer is only at risk for the face amount minus the cash value. Partial surrenders and separate accounts are not features of whole life policies.

9. A: A payor benefit is a disability rider for the policyowner which waives the policy premium in the event of the death or disability of the payor of the premium. It does not provide any type of life insurance coverage for the payor. While the policyowner is entitled to take out a loan on the policy, usually after three years, it does not provide for interest-free repayment of a loan.

10. B: The Health Insurance Portability and Accountability Act of 1996 (HIPAA) consists of five separate titles governing the portability of health care and preexisting conditions, health care fraud, pre-tax medical spending accounts, group health care plans, and company-owned life insurance plans. Title II specifically addresses standards and rules regarding the handling of patient medical information.

11. B: Most whole life, universal life, and variable universal life policies offer a living needs rider that will pay out a portion of the death benefit when certain conditions are met, such as terminal illness of the insured. Term policies, however, are considered temporary insurance and do not offer these benefits.

12. A: Contact lenses and prescription lenses are covered under all vision insurance plans, in addition to annual eye examinations. Safety glasses and lost, stolen, or broken lenses and frames are not covered. Eye injuries and diseases of the eye are covered under medical insurance plans only.

13. D: Group life insurance policies are written as a single term policy, usually on an annual and renewable basis. These policies do not build cash value. Employees who pay a portion of the premium are usually given a choice on the amount of coverage to select, which is often based on a multiple of their annual salary. This coverage usually includes a fixed amount of coverage for an employee's spouse and children. Most group life insurance policies offer the ability to convert this coverage to a permanent whole life policy upon retirement.

14. C: Most short-term disability policies have an elimination period, which is known as a time deductible. The elimination period normally begins on the date of the injury, as long as the injury date is certified by a doctor's report. In this case, benefits would begin paying on March 24, 14 days after the injury. Insurers normally require that the insured notify the insurer of a pending claim or loss within 20 days or as soon as reasonably possible. This notification can be provided by the insured, an insured's provider, or an insurance agent. Insurers may have other reporting requirements. For example, an insurer may set periodic reporting requirements for a continuing disability.

15. B: A carryover provision in an insurance contract allows an insured to carry over a portion of their expenses incurred in the last three months of the current year to apply toward next year's deductible. This reduces the amount that the insured has to pay out of pocket. Carryover provisions are more common with employer-sponsored health plans and do add to the cost of the monthly premium.

16. B: While a group's overall claims history is used to help set the rates of a group health plan, the health history of the group or individuals within the group is not typically used as a determining rating factor. Since the insurer is primarily concerned with maintaining an adverse selection when determining rates, personnel turnover is considered. The group's industry classification (type of work performed) is also considered.

17. B: An insurer can reinstate a lapsed policy at its discretion as long as the policyowner pays all of the back premiums plus interest. The insured may be required to provide proof of insurability with a new application. In this case, the insurer has 45 days to reject the application; otherwise, the policy will automatically be put back into effect.

18. A: Annuities are not bank-issued savings instruments and are therefore not insured by the Federal Deposit Insurance Corporation (FDIC). Indexed annuities are guaranteed only by the issuing insurance or financial company. The issuing company guarantees the principal and guarantees that the annual rate of return will never drop below 0 percent. Returns for indexed annuities are timed to a major stock index, usually the Standard and Poor's 500 Index (S&P 500). These annuities offer tax-deferred growth.

19. A: The elimination period of a disability policy can also be considered a time deductible. The time deductible that an insured selects between an accident or injury and the time that the insurer provides benefits has a direct impact on the cost of the policy. The longer the time deductible selected, the lower the cost of the policy. Disability policies usually have longer time deductibles for covered illnesses but shorter time deductibles for accidents.

20. A: Sworn statements regarding an insured's health can only be made by a physician, otherwise known as an attending physician's report. Observations made by the insurance agent are a vital component of field underwriting and are used in determining the current health of an insured. Credit reports are also used by underwriters to determine whether or not to issue a life insurance policy.

21. C: The 30-day probationary period on Paul's health plan would begin on the date of the application. The primary purpose of a probationary period is to prevent individuals from obtaining health insurance coverage for preexisting illnesses (as opposed to known preexisting conditions) and help prevent fraud. Health insurance companies can set up to a 90-day maximum probationary period.

22. A: Any benefits paid through a long-term care rider are subtracted from the death benefit, thereby reducing the face amount payable upon the death of the insured. The insured would normally have to demonstrate the inability to perform two out of six daily tasks before qualifying for benefits to be paid. Once qualified, the policy will pay up to the entire face amount. All benefits paid are income tax-free.

23. C: The insurer would adjust the policy face amount to pay what the paid policy premiums would have purchased at the insured's corrected age. If the age misstatement was greater than the insured's correct age, the insurer is only required to refund the corrected premium difference. Insurers do not withdraw cash value from the policy to make this type of correction. The insurer cannot cancel a policy for this reason after the two-year contestability period, nor can they require the insured to pay the premium difference, as the premium amount is set in the policy contract.

24. C: Only the lump sum death benefit settlement option is completely income tax-free. All other settlement options will generate interest as their proceeds are paid out, which is considered taxable income. The principal death benefit amount is nontaxable.

25. B: Universal life and variable life policies feature both a general and a separate account. Term insurance only has a general account since it does not offer interest or investment options to the insured. Since all of the policy risk is assumed by the insured, variable universal life policies only have a separate account and do not have a general account from which the insurer guarantees the death benefit or policy values.

26. D: Medicare supplement (Medigap) policies are no longer allowed to offer prescription drug benefits on new policies. Prescription coverage would need to be obtained under a Medicare Part D prescription plan. Medicare Parts A and B are prerequisites for purchasing a Medicare supplement plan. These plans are sold and administered by private insurance companies, so the monthly premium is paid to the insurer.

Medicare supplement policies also provide for health care outside the US, where Medicare does not.

27. C: Medicare Advantage plans, also referred to as Medicare Part C, are managed health care plans paid by Medicare to offer a complete health care solution for Medicare enrollees. Many Medicare Advantage plans also include Part D prescription drug benefits without a deductible. Insureds are required to use doctors and services within the plan's network, much like HMO plans.

28. A: A disability income policy that only requires the insured's inability to perform the main duties of their own occupation is the least restrictive in terms of qualifying for benefits. This disability definition normally requires the highest premium. Policies can also be written that require the insured's inability to perform any occupation, consequently making it harder to qualify for benefits. Total and/or permanent disability income policies require that the insured is not able to work again in order to qualify for benefits.

29. D: Life insurance replacement laws protect the insured against unnecessary costs and risks. It is the insurance agent's responsibility to determine whether the new life insurance policy is being written to replace an older policy with similar coverage. Canceling a life insurance policy in the past is not a consideration when determining what is in the best interest of the insured. Questions regarding the suitability of a new policy may arise if an insured has other pending insurance applications or has recently taken out loans against one or more existing policies which may be used to fund a new policy.

30. A: A partial withdrawal from a universal life policy will not necessarily affect the face amount of the policy, as it is considered a withdrawal of the policy's cash value. Some universal life policies offer a reduction of the death benefit with partial withdrawals to offset the cash value withdrawal. Otherwise, removing too much cash value may put the policy at risk of lapse. Insurers offer grace periods and policy reinstatements for late payment of premiums, which would not affect the policy's face amount. Also, policy loans and riders will not reduce a policy's face amount.

31. A: Spendthrift laws were created with the intention of protecting the death benefit of an insurance policy against creditors of either the insured or the beneficiary. In most cases, a beneficiary can only receive this type of protection if the policyowner selected a settlement option other than a lump sum payment where the insurance company holds the principal.

32. D: The insurer would only be required to pay benefits after the two-year contestability period of the policy. The contestability period allows an insurer to contest and void an insurance contract within the first two years of the policy issue date if they can demonstrate that there was a material misstatement or concealment of facts that would have caused the insurer not to issue the policy had it been known at the time. An insured's suicide can also be contested within this two-year period.

33. C: The performance of the cash value in an indexed universal life (IUL) policy is tied to a specific stock index, usually the S&P 500. While indexed universal life policies do not offer a guaranteed rate of return on the cash value of the policy, they do guarantee against loss in the event of a market downturn. Most IUL policies will cap the annualized rate of return at a specific amount. Term life policies do not have a cash value component. Whole life policies offer a fixed rate of return, while variable life policies are tied to investments which can lose value.

127

34. D: Since Kathy is covered under both a Medicare Advantage plan and her husband's health care plan, her Medicare Advantage plan would pick up most of the cost of the surgery. Medicare determined this coordination of benefits since her husband's employer health care plan covers less than 20 employees. If her husband's plan covered more than 20 employees, it would pay the majority of the cost of surgery in this case.

35. A: A contract of adhesion means that the contract is completely created and worded by one party, to which the other party has no input and can only accept or reject the terms. Contracts such as life insurance are contracts of adhesion. The benefit of this type of contract to a policyholder is that the writer of the contract is responsible for any ambiguities in wording from a legal perspective. The policyowner has no input and cannot negotiate any of its wording, details, or provisions. In this case the insurance company would be forced to pay, since no wording in the contract spelled out what constituted a dangerous activity.

36. C: A home improvement loan is not a contract based upon chance or a random act and therefore does not fit the definition of an aleatory contract. An aleatory contract requires that certain events occur that are beyond the control of either party. All types of insurance can be considered aleatory contracts. A lottery ticket can also be considered an aleatory contract since winning the lottery is based solely upon chance.

37. D: Short-term medical insurance is designed as a stand-alone policy that can provide coverage for as little as 30 days up to 3 months. It will not supplement or provide any additional coverage to a major medical plan. Short-term health plans should not be considered a true replacement for major medical plans, as they often do not cover preexisting conditions, are not guaranteed issue plans, and may not be renewable. However, short-term plans do make sense in some cases, providing for health insurance coverage when no other options are available.

38. A: A key employee insurance policy will pay the policyowner in the event that a key employee becomes disabled. Although the benefits are received tax-free by the business, the premiums paid for the policy by the business are not tax-deductible. While a key employee is disabled, the policy will pay the business for loss of revenue and can be used to hire and train a replacement employee.

39. D: The death benefit proceeds of a life insurance policy will become part of the insured's estate upon death if a named beneficiary has not been set up previously. This can and often does lead to probate court, in which an insured's creditors may try to lay claim to the death benefit proceeds. The purpose of creating a named beneficiary is for the death benefit to be paid solely to the beneficiary income tax-free and to avoid probate.

40. D: Annuity contracts are sold without any upfront fees. The insurance company recoups its expenses and commissions paid to the agent as it earns investment returns above what is guaranteed in the annuity contract in what is referred to as the back-end load. Surrender changes are put in place in the annuity contract to cover these expenses should the annuitant wish to withdrawal their principal early. Surrender charges can be as high was 10 percent during the first year and decrease annually until the end of the surrender charge period as detailed in the annuity contract.

41. A: In order to properly set rates, insurers must be able to predict the risk of loss based upon large amounts of historical and statistical data, often referred to as the law of large numbers. Any type of loss, natural or accidental, must be unexpected and solely due to chance. Since those individuals that are at the highest risk of loss tend to be the ones more likely to seek insurance coverage, insurers rely on randomly selecting exposures to prevent this adverse selection from taking place.

42. A: Each state has its own laws and regulations governing the administration of workers' compensation insurance. Workers' compensation plans are underwritten by private insurance companies who group similar classes of businesses together and base their rates on a five-year loss history within these separate classes. Workers' compensation insurance is required by law for any type of business that has employees.

43. C: A rating on an insurance policy represents a substandard but acceptable risk to the insurance company, who will issue a policy with a higher premium as a result. Insurers use rating classifications to determine which risks to insure in addition to the appropriate premium to charge for those risks. It is important that the insurance agent explain to an insured why a particular policy is rated with a higher premium than was originally quoted.

44. D: A policyowner must be able to demonstrate that an insurable interest exists for the life of an insured at the time the policy is written. This is to prevent any moral hazard or fraud at the hands of the policyholder against the life of an insured. The policyowner is not required to demonstrate this insurable interest at a later date, including at the time of death of the insured or after the two-year contestability period.

45. A: The IRS uses the 7-pay test on life insurance policies to ensure that the amount paid into a life insurance policy during the first seven years does not exceed the actual cost of insurance relative to the policy death benefit. If a life insurance policy does not pass this 7-pay test, an insurer can refund the additional premiums to prevent this. If these premiums are not refunded within 60 days after year-end of a failed test, the policy will be considered a modified endowment contract (MEC). The IRS will treat all payments from the policy on a last-in, first-out (LIFO) basis, and the proceeds will be taxed as ordinary income, much like an IRA. A 10 percent penalty will also be incurred if the policyowner is less than 59 ½ years of age.

46. C: Policy loans that are not paid back at the insured's time of death are subtracted with interest from the face amount. Policy loans are secured through the cash value of the policy and do not affect the policy's cash value since loans are paid back with interest. Loans are usually not available until the policy has been in effect for three years.

47. A: Nonforfeiture options in a life insurance contract guarantee the cash value of the contract in the event that the policy lapses due to nonpayment. These options include the cash surrender value, which can be paid to the policyowner in a lump sum. Other options include a reduced paid-up policy, paid in full with the cash proceeds, or extended term insurance coverage which will extend coverage until the cash value resources are exhausted.

48. B: The usual, reasonable, and customary (URC) fee schedule is set by determining the average fee charged by all providers in a given geographical area. Fees that are charged outside of this UCR schedule are often the insured's responsibility to pay. Pre-negotiated fees are a feature of preferred provider organizations (PPOs) but normally do not extend to standard health care plans.

49. B: Life settlements allow an insured to sell their life insurance contract to a third party in exchange for a lump sum payment. In a life settlement, any amount received greater than the premiums paid into the policy is considered taxable income. All of the other options are generally considered good reasons for considering a life settlement on a life insurance policy.

50. B: A change in occupation on a health insurance policy can either increase or decrease the premium based upon the type of work being performed. If an insured moves from a less dangerous line of work to an occupation deemed more dangerous, the insurer would most likely increase the premium due to the increased risk. If a claim is made and the insured is now in a riskier line of work than was originally reported, the insurer will pay only according to what the original premium would have provided. If an insured moves from a more dangerous to a less dangerous type of work, the insurer would normally reduce the premium amount and return the excess unearned premium from the date that the insured's job had changed.

51. D: The amount of premium paid by the insured and the frequency of payments are included in the consideration clause of the contract and are not included in the insuring clause. The insuring clause outlines the parties to the contract as well as the promise to pay upon being provided with the proof of loss.

52. A: A common reason to create an irrevocable beneficiary to a life insurance policy is a divorce settlement, where a court may require the policyowner to make the policyowner's spouse an irrevocable beneficiary. In this case, the policyowner is required by the court to keep the policy in force and is limited from taking out a policy loan in most cases. A bankruptcy court may require a policyowner to surrender a portion of the cash value of a life insurance policy in some cases but will not require an irrevocable beneficiary to be created. Medicare also cannot require that an irrevocable beneficiary be created. There is rarely a need to create an irrevocable beneficiary for a juvenile policy.

53. C: An accidental death and dismemberment policy would be the best option. Accidental death and dismemberment policies are lower in cost than traditional life policies since the insured is not required to qualify medically. AD&D policies do share some of the restrictions of other policy types, such as other listed dangerous hobbies and accidents while under the influence of drugs or alcohol.

54. B: In most states, the policy free look period exists for 10 days from the date that the policy was delivered to the policyowner. A receipt of policy delivery must be issued on the delivery date of the policy to the policyowner.

55. C: The three types of policy maximum benefit limits are lifetime, annual, and per-cause. The Affordable Care Act (ACA) prevents insurance companies from limiting coverage amounts for essential health services such as outpatient care, hospitalization and emergency services, mental health and substance abuse disorders, and prescription drugs, to name a few.

56. B: Most insurance companies utilize an MIB report to determine an insured's medical history. The MIB Group (formerly known as Medical Information Bureau) collects medical information from several sources, including member insurers, to determine the accuracy of medical information supplied as part of a life insurance application. This information is available to consumers upon request.

57. B: The Uniform Simultaneous Death Act states that when an insured and primary beneficiary die as a result of the same occurrence and their order of death cannot be determined, it will be assumed that the insured died last. This serves to protect the secondary beneficiaries. Therefore, in this case, it would be assumed that each insured died last, and the policies would be paid to their respective secondary beneficiaries.

58. C: Traveling to a politically unstable country or region is not considered a typical policy exclusion unless an actual war has been declared and an insured's death is a result of that war. Piloting an aircraft, as well as other hazardous occupations or hobbies, are typical exclusions.

Suicide is specifically excluded during the first two years of a policy contract, after which it falls outside of the contestability period for the insurer.

59. A: Term policies, variable life, and indexed universal life policies all offer a guaranteed minimum death benefit. With a variable universal life policy, all of the investment risk, including the death benefit, is not guaranteed by the insurer.

60. D: Policy representations are assertions of fact that are believed to be true and do not represent actual warranties, which are promises made to be true as stated in the contract. If the initial premium was not collected at the time of the application, an agent must collect the first premium. In addition to the premium, the agent will normally have the insured sign a statement of no loss, testifying that their overall health has not dramatically changed. At this point the contract is delivered to the insured, and the agent obtains the delivery receipt.

61. D: Viatical settlements are designed for terminally ill insured policyowners to sell their life insurance policy for less than the face amount in order to pay for current expenses. Viatical settlement providers must offer an amount more than the cash surrender value and more than any living needs benefits that the policy may provide. In this case, the living needs benefit of the policy will allow the insured to receive at least 70 percent and up to 90 percent of the policy face amount prior to death without any additional fees or penalties. Viatical settlement offers do not include related expenses and commissions paid to brokers for this service.

62. C: All four options can be offered as riders to a whole life policy. An accidental death and dismemberment rider can double or triple the policy face amount in the event of an accidental death or loss of limbs. Guaranteed insurability offers the insured the ability to purchase additional insurance at specified intervals. A return of premium rider increases the death benefit, providing term insurance equal to all premiums paid into the policy. A disability income rider waives the premium after a standard waiting period if the insured becomes totally disabled and pays the insured a monthly income but does not change the face amount payable to the insured upon death.

63. C: According to the IRS, policyowners are entitled to receive the life insurance face amount on a tax-free basis upon the death of the insured. This tax-free treatment also applies to any living needs or other accelerated death benefits that have been previously paid. If a life insurance policy is surrendered, sold, or no longer passes the modified endowment contract 7-pay test, any amount of money received greater than the premiums paid into the contract is considered taxable income by the IRS.

64. B: Not revealing a previous cancer diagnosis would be considered a material misstatement by an insured on a life insurance policy application. An insurer could deny a claim and contest the policy contract if the insured died of cancer within two years of the policy issue date. All of the other answers can be considered immaterial misrepresentations. Although any of these could be the reason an insurer would deny a policy application, they could not be considered as reasons to deny paying a life insurance claim at any time once the policy has been issued.

65. D: HMO health plans are limited to a particular geographical region. Coverage is only provided outside of the geographical area in the event of an emergency. A standard major medical plan would not be limited to a particular geographical area, giving an insured the freedom to obtain coverage wherever it is needed. Under a PPO or a POS (point of sale) plan, insureds are not restricted from medical and health care services obtained outside of their network. However, this may increase the fees and deductibles that the insured is required to pay. Specialized health care services usually require a referral from the insured's primary care physician in order to qualify for the lowest rates and deductibles.

66. D: Replacing an insurance policy may make sense for the insured in some cases. For instance, an insured has a term policy but wants to replace the policy with one that builds cash value and is willing to accept the risk of variable investments. In the other examples provided, an insured usually would be better served by purchasing additional insurance rather than replacing an existing policy.

67. B: Automatic premium loans will automatically borrow against the cash value of the policy in order to pay the monthly premium. This option, if chosen by the policyowner, will borrow the past due premium amount from the policy cash value on the last day of the grace period to prevent the policy from lapsing due to nonpayment.

68. C: A business overhead expense policy pays for business-related expenses such as rent, utilities, and labor costs if the business owner were to become disabled. This type of policy does not cover the loss of income for the business owner. Such coverage may be available through a group disability policy. Disability buyout policies are designed to enable the purchase of a disabled or deceased owner's share of the business by other business owners. Business continuation insurance covers the life or disability of a business partner in order to provide needed funds to continue the business without disruption.

69. C: Typical major medical insurance plans, commonly defined as 80/20 plans, pay 80 percent of health care expenses after the annual deductible has been met. In this case, the insured would first pay the $500 annual deductible before the insurance benefits take effect. Of the remaining $1,500, the insurance company would cover 80 percent or $1,200, leaving the remaining $300 as the insured's responsibility, for a total of $800 out of pocket.

70. D: The Affordable Care Act (ACA) passed by Congress in 2010 prevents insurers from denying coverage for preexisting conditions. It also prevents insurers from charging different rates for men and women. Certain private health care plans sold and in force before March 23, 2010, that are considered grandfathered health care plans, do allow for the exclusion of some preexisting conditions, provided that the primary structure and cost of these plans does not dramatically change.

71. C: The minimum grace period for a monthly premium insurance policy is 10 days before a policy can be considered lapsed. For a policy paid weekly, the minimum period is 7 days. Insurers normally will require a statement of health to be completed when accepting late payments on a lapsed policy and may attach late fees as well.

72. C: Generally, premiums paid for LTC insurance are not tax-deductible unless the amount of premiums paid exceeds 7.5 percent of an insured's annual adjusted gross income. However, all benefits are received income tax-free. Policies are guaranteed renewable as long as the premium is paid. LTC benefits, usually paid on a per-day basis, are designed to protect one's assets from being completely consumed by LTC costs.

73. C: In this case, the insured met their $3,000 yearly deductible but did not meet their annual out-of-pocket limit of $6,500. The insurance company in this case would pay 80 percent or $12,800 of the remaining $16,000 balance, while the insured would pay their coinsurance amount of 20 percent or $3,200.

74. A: Qualified retirement plans are funded with pre-tax dollars, meaning that no income tax is paid on either employer or employee contributions. All withdrawals are considered taxable income. An employer with a qualified retirement plan must provide equal retirement benefits to all eligible employees, usually after one year of full-time employment. The employer must also have a vesting schedule whereby the employee will fully own any contributions to the plan made by their employer.

75. C: Part III of the insurance application constitutes the agent's report. The agent is the only representative from the insurance company that is able to see and hear the insured. It is the agent's responsibility to observe and record any and all information that he or she feels would be pertinent to accurately evaluate the risk to be insured.

76. C: Policy owners can take out tax-free loans without having to give up any of the death benefit on the policy. The cash value of the policy is used as collateral for the loan. If the policyowner chooses not to pay back the loan, the loan amount is deducted from the face value of the policy at the time of death. However, if the policy is surrendered, the loan is considered taxable income.

77. B: A single premium policy has immediate cash value, whereas the other premium payment options can take up to three years to begin generating cash value. The interest credited to the immediate cash value generates additional cash value at a much faster rate. A single premium policy therefore has the ability to pay its own premiums much sooner and thus represents a lower total premium outlay over the life of the policy.

78. D: Under the ownership provision in an insurance policy, only the policyowner has rights in the policy. The insured only has rights if they are also the policyowner. The policyowner has exclusive rights to change beneficiaries, settlement options, ownership, etc. Beneficiaries do not have any rights in a policy contract.

79. D: Some term life insurance policies offer both a renewable and a convertible option. The renewable option allows the insured to continue the policy on the renewal date without providing evidence of insurability based upon attained age at the time of renewal. The convertible option allows the insured to convert a term policy to a whole life policy based upon the insured's attained age at the time of conversion only. Therefore, both renewable and convertible options can only be exercised based on the insured's attained age.

80. B: Many cancer policies severely limit or do not cover outpatient treatment. As a result, the $2,900 outpatient treatment would most likely be the patient's responsibility. Adding the $1,000 deductible would bring the insurance company's responsibility to $35,600. Also, most cancer policies do not cover cancer-related illnesses such as influenza or pneumonia. Cancer policies do cover most inpatient procedures, including but not limited to chemotherapy, hospital stays, x-rays, and prescription drugs.

81. C: The consideration clause is an essential item that makes up any contract. It outlines the responsibility of the insured to make timely payments and provides the amount of each payment. In exchange of premium, the insurer will provide the agreed-upon coverage. Exclusions, policyowner rights, and acknowledgments of truthfulness by the insured are addressed in other parts of the policy contract.

82. D: A unilateral contract is a contract in which only one party is obligated to perform in exchange for consideration, or money. Insurance contracts are contracts of adhesion as a result of being unilateral contracts, meaning that only the performing party drafts all provisions of the contract. All insurance contracts are considered aleatory, meaning that they rely solely upon chance events.

83. C: Most insurers will use a person's race as a consideration only as it relates to medical history. However, insurers are prohibited from denying risks based upon race. The life insurance underwriting process can utilize personal interviews with friends, family members, and other acquaintances in addition to medical records, driving records, credit history, claims history for all insurance types, etc. in order to determine the insurability and classification of a risk.

84. B: Reassignment is not a life insurance settlement option. A fixed period option provides for the beneficiary to receive guaranteed, set payments for a fixed period of time after the death of the insured. An interest-only settlement option only pays out the interest accrued from the face amount for a set period of time before the policy face amount is paid. A life income settlement option purchases an annuity for the beneficiary with the insurance proceeds that can be paid out to the beneficiary in a variety of ways as chosen by the policyholder.

85. D: All four options can be offered as riders to a whole life policy. Guaranteed insurability offers the insured the ability to purchase additional insurance at specified intervals. A cost-of-living rider enables an insured to purchase additional insurance yearly to offset inflation. A return of cash value rider provides term insurance equal to a policy's cash value in addition to the policy face amount. A waiver of premium rider pays the premium after a standard waiting period if the insured becomes totally disabled. It will continue to pay the premiums as long as the insured is totally disabled or until the death of the insured.

86. C: The insured would have been issued a conditional binding receipt upon completing the application and paying the initial premium. In this case, the insurance company would have been required to pay both the policy face amount and the accidental death benefit, since it most likely would've issued the policy based on the insured's health and medical history. If the insurer discovered information that would have resulted in them denying the policy application, the claim would have been denied and the initial premium returned.

87. C: The relation of earnings to insurance clause states that an insured cannot profit off an insurance contract, regardless of the amount of insurance or the premium paid. If it is determined that the insured would potentially profit from a disability contract, the amount of coverage would be adjusted to the percentage outlined in the contract, and the excess premium would be returned to the insured.

88. B: All of the life insurance policies listed can be used to pay the balance of a mortgage in the event the insured dies prematurely. However, a credit life policy offers decreasing term insurance protection that reduces the amount of coverage as the mortgage balance decreases, which makes it the most appropriate type of policy for mortgage protection.

89. A: A weekly premium payment plan would be the most expensive mode of payment for an insurance policy, as each payment, regardless of how often it occurs, represents a cost to the insurer. The method of payment chosen, such as an automatic bank draft, may offset these added expenses. The policyowner can change the premium payment mode at any time.

90. C: Age and gender are rating factors used when determining life insurance rates but are not material to the issuance of the policy. In this case, the only difference was the gender selected. The insurance company would most likely refund the premium difference that rating her as male produced, since insurers tend to rate males higher than females of the same age when determining rates.

91. C: A representation is considered an implied statement that a party believes to be true at the time the statement is made. If certain investment returns were guaranteed in writing in the contract to be true, they would be considered warranties. Projections and expectations are a part of any type of variable investment, which is why strict rules governing how variable contracts can be marketed and represented exist. These rules also extend to any printed materials used in the presentation to an insured.

92. C: The only two basic types of joint life insurance death benefits are joint life and joint survivorship. A joint life policy insures two or more people and is payable upon the first insured to die. A joint survivorship death benefit covers the lives of all insureds and is payable upon the last to die. Neither the joint ownership nor joint insured option describes the death benefit.

93. B: In 2022, the individual limit that one can contribute is $3,650, or $7,300 for married couples, so in this case, the account balance would be $16,150 since this employee is not married. Insureds must be enrolled in a high deductible health plan in order to qualify for a health savings account (HSA). The primary benefit of an HSA is that any unused funds at year's end can be rolled over to the next year without penalty. Funds used for non-qualified medical expenses prior to age 65 are subject to a 20 percent tax penalty by the IRS.

94. D: Mutual insurance companies are owned by their policyholders as opposed to stock insurance companies owned by shareholders. Mutual insurers will pay dividends to their policyholders, which represent a return of premium. If these dividends are continually set to accumulate at interest, the cash value of the policy will grow at a faster rate due to compounding interest.

95. B: Once a notice of a claim has been filed with an insurer, the insured must wait 60 days before any legal action can be taken against an insurance company. Typically, an insured has up to 3 years after the 60-day waiting period to take legal action. The time limit for an insured to bring legal action may vary from state to state.

96. A: Since the policyowner can make all decisions regarding the ownership of a life insurance contract, the insured would not need to consent to or be notified of a policy replacement. Life insurance companies and agents are required by law to provide a Notice of Replacement not only to a policyholder but to the existing insurance company that a policy is being replaced. This is to protect the rights of the policyholder, since replacing an existing life insurance contract with another is not always in the policyholder's best interests. The cost of insurance increases with age, and the new policy will require a new two-year contestability period. It may also require proof of insurability for the insured.

97. B: A terminated employee normally has up to 60 days from the date of termination to elect COBRA coverage. In this instance, the employee's termination date would've been July 15th. The Consolidated Omnibus Budget Reconciliation Act (COBRA) outlines specific regulations for employers with 20 or more employees, who are no longer eligible to participate in a group health plan, for the temporary continuation of health insurance. State laws and/or unique circumstances may extend this window to elect coverage beyond the normal 60 days.

98. D: Social Security determines retirement eligibility through the use of an earned credits system. Normally, a person must have 40 earned credits (equal to 10 years) to become eligible to receive full retirement benefits. Indexed monthly earnings are calculated using a person's highest 35 years of earnings. A person's estimated retirement earnings can be obtained through the Social Security Administration.

99. D: One of the features of a universal life policy is a guaranteed death benefit. Although an adjustable face amount and flexible premiums are shared by both universal life and variable life policies, only variable life and variable universal life policies offer investment options.

100. D: Insurers will only provide coverage for newborns 14 days after birth. A child rider on a whole life policy consists of level term coverage for one or more children. The insurer will normally allow covered children to convert this coverage to a whole life policy, usually at age 21 or 25, without requiring evidence of insurability.

How to Overcome Test Anxiety

Just the thought of taking a test is enough to make most people a little nervous. A test is an important event that can have a long-term impact on your future, so it's important to take it seriously and it's natural to feel anxious about performing well. But just because anxiety is normal, that doesn't mean that it's helpful in test taking, or that you should simply accept it as part of your life. Anxiety can have a variety of effects. These effects can be mild, like making you feel slightly nervous, or severe, like blocking your ability to focus or remember even a simple detail.

If you experience test anxiety—whether severe or mild—it's important to know how to beat it. To discover this, first you need to understand what causes test anxiety.

Causes of Test Anxiety

While we often think of anxiety as an uncontrollable emotional state, it can actually be caused by simple, practical things. One of the most common causes of test anxiety is that a person does not feel adequately prepared for their test. This feeling can be the result of many different issues such as poor study habits or lack of organization, but the most common culprit is time management. Starting to study too late, failing to organize your study time to cover all of the material, or being distracted while you study will mean that you're not well prepared for the test. This may lead to cramming the night before, which will cause you to be physically and mentally exhausted for the test. Poor time management also contributes to feelings of stress, fear, and hopelessness as you realize you are not well prepared but don't know what to do about it.

Other times, test anxiety is not related to your preparation for the test but comes from unresolved fear. This may be a past failure on a test, or poor performance on tests in general. It may come from comparing yourself to others who seem to be performing better or from the stress of living up to expectations. Anxiety may be driven by fears of the future—how failure on this test would affect your educational and career goals. These fears are often completely irrational, but they can still negatively impact your test performance.

> **Review Video: 3 Reasons You Have Test Anxiety**
> Visit mometrix.com/academy and enter code: 428468

137

Elements of Test Anxiety

As mentioned earlier, test anxiety is considered to be an emotional state, but it has physical and mental components as well. Sometimes you may not even realize that you are suffering from test anxiety until you notice the physical symptoms. These can include trembling hands, rapid heartbeat, sweating, nausea, and tense muscles. Extreme anxiety may lead to fainting or vomiting. Obviously, any of these symptoms can have a negative impact on testing. It is important to recognize them as soon as they begin to occur so that you can address the problem before it damages your performance.

> **Review Video: 3 Ways to Tell You Have Test Anxiety**
> Visit mometrix.com/academy and enter code: 927847

The mental components of test anxiety include trouble focusing and inability to remember learned information. During a test, your mind is on high alert, which can help you recall information and stay focused for an extended period of time. However, anxiety interferes with your mind's natural processes, causing you to blank out, even on the questions you know well. The strain of testing during anxiety makes it difficult to stay focused, especially on a test that may take several hours. Extreme anxiety can take a huge mental toll, making it difficult not only to recall test information but even to understand the test questions or pull your thoughts together.

> **Review Video: How Test Anxiety Affects Memory**
> Visit mometrix.com/academy and enter code: 609003

Effects of Test Anxiety

Test anxiety is like a disease—if left untreated, it will get progressively worse. Anxiety leads to poor performance, and this reinforces the feelings of fear and failure, which in turn lead to poor performances on subsequent tests. It can grow from a mild nervousness to a crippling condition. If allowed to progress, test anxiety can have a big impact on your schooling, and consequently on your future.

Test anxiety can spread to other parts of your life. Anxiety on tests can become anxiety in any stressful situation, and blanking on a test can turn into panicking in a job situation. But fortunately, you don't have to let anxiety rule your testing and determine your grades. There are a number of relatively simple steps you can take to move past anxiety and function normally on a test and in the rest of life.

> **Review Video: How Test Anxiety Impacts Your Grades**
> Visit mometrix.com/academy and enter code: 939819

Physical Steps for Beating Test Anxiety

While test anxiety is a serious problem, the good news is that it can be overcome. It doesn't have to control your ability to think and remember information. While it may take time, you can begin taking steps today to beat anxiety.

Just as your first hint that you may be struggling with anxiety comes from the physical symptoms, the first step to treating it is also physical. Rest is crucial for having a clear, strong mind. If you are tired, it is much easier to give in to anxiety. But if you establish good sleep habits, your body and mind will be ready to perform optimally, without the strain of exhaustion. Additionally, sleeping well helps you to retain information better, so you're more likely to recall the answers when you see the test questions.

Getting good sleep means more than going to bed on time. It's important to allow your brain time to relax. Take study breaks from time to time so it doesn't get overworked, and don't study right before bed. Take time to rest your mind before trying to rest your body, or you may find it difficult to fall asleep.

> **Review Video: <u>The Importance of Sleep for Your Brain</u>**
> Visit mometrix.com/academy and enter code: 319338

Along with sleep, other aspects of physical health are important in preparing for a test. Good nutrition is vital for good brain function. Sugary foods and drinks may give a burst of energy but this burst is followed by a crash, both physically and emotionally. Instead, fuel your body with protein and vitamin-rich foods.

Also, drink plenty of water. Dehydration can lead to headaches and exhaustion, especially if your brain is already under stress from the rigors of the test. Particularly if your test is a long one, drink water during the breaks. And if possible, take an energy-boosting snack to eat between sections.

> **Review Video: <u>How Diet Can Affect your Mood</u>**
> Visit mometrix.com/academy and enter code: 624317

Along with sleep and diet, a third important part of physical health is exercise. Maintaining a steady workout schedule is helpful, but even taking 5-minute study breaks to walk can help get your blood pumping faster and clear your head. Exercise also releases endorphins, which contribute to a positive feeling and can help combat test anxiety.

When you nurture your physical health, you are also contributing to your mental health. If your body is healthy, your mind is much more likely to be healthy as well. So take time to rest, nourish your body with healthy food and water, and get moving as much as possible. Taking these physical steps will make you stronger and more able to take the mental steps necessary to overcome test anxiety.

Mental Steps for Beating Test Anxiety

Working on the mental side of test anxiety can be more challenging, but as with the physical side, there are clear steps you can take to overcome it. As mentioned earlier, test anxiety often stems from lack of preparation, so the obvious solution is to prepare for the test. Effective studying may be the most important weapon you have for beating test anxiety, but you can and should employ several other mental tools to combat fear.

First, boost your confidence by reminding yourself of past success—tests or projects that you aced. If you're putting as much effort into preparing for this test as you did for those, there's no reason you should expect to fail here. Work hard to prepare; then trust your preparation.

Second, surround yourself with encouraging people. It can be helpful to find a study group, but be sure that the people you're around will encourage a positive attitude. If you spend time with others who are anxious or cynical, this will only contribute to your own anxiety. Look for others who are motivated to study hard from a desire to succeed, not from a fear of failure.

Third, reward yourself. A test is physically and mentally tiring, even without anxiety, and it can be helpful to have something to look forward to. Plan an activity following the test, regardless of the outcome, such as going to a movie or getting ice cream.

When you are taking the test, if you find yourself beginning to feel anxious, remind yourself that you know the material. Visualize successfully completing the test. Then take a few deep, relaxing breaths and return to it. Work through the questions carefully but with confidence, knowing that you are capable of succeeding.

Developing a healthy mental approach to test taking will also aid in other areas of life. Test anxiety affects more than just the actual test—it can be damaging to your mental health and even contribute to depression. It's important to beat test anxiety before it becomes a problem for more than testing.

> **Review Video: Test Anxiety and Depression**
> Visit mometrix.com/academy and enter code: 904704

Study Strategy

Being prepared for the test is necessary to combat anxiety, but what does being prepared look like? You may study for hours on end and still not feel prepared. What you need is a strategy for test prep. The next few pages outline our recommended steps to help you plan out and conquer the challenge of preparation.

STEP 1: SCOPE OUT THE TEST

Learn everything you can about the format (multiple choice, essay, etc.) and what will be on the test. Gather any study materials, course outlines, or sample exams that may be available. Not only will this help you to prepare, but knowing what to expect can help to alleviate test anxiety.

STEP 2: MAP OUT THE MATERIAL

Look through the textbook or study guide and make note of how many chapters or sections it has. Then divide these over the time you have. For example, if a book has 15 chapters and you have five days to study, you need to cover three chapters each day. Even better, if you have the time, leave an extra day at the end for overall review after you have gone through the material in depth.

If time is limited, you may need to prioritize the material. Look through it and make note of which sections you think you already have a good grasp on, and which need review. While you are studying, skim quickly through the familiar sections and take more time on the challenging parts. Write out your plan so you don't get lost as you go. Having a written plan also helps you feel more in control of the study, so anxiety is less likely to arise from feeling overwhelmed at the amount to cover.

STEP 3: GATHER YOUR TOOLS

Decide what study method works best for you. Do you prefer to highlight in the book as you study and then go back over the highlighted portions? Or do you type out notes of the important information? Or is it helpful to make flashcards that you can carry with you? Assemble the pens, index cards, highlighters, post-it notes, and any other materials you may need so you won't be distracted by getting up to find things while you study.

If you're having a hard time retaining the information or organizing your notes, experiment with different methods. For example, try color-coding by subject with colored pens, highlighters, or post-it notes. If you learn better by hearing, try recording yourself reading your notes so you can listen while in the car, working out, or simply sitting at your desk. Ask a friend to quiz you from your flashcards, or try teaching someone the material to solidify it in your mind.

STEP 4: CREATE YOUR ENVIRONMENT

It's important to avoid distractions while you study. This includes both the obvious distractions like visitors and the subtle distractions like an uncomfortable chair (or a too-comfortable couch that makes you want to fall asleep). Set up the best study environment possible: good lighting and a comfortable work area. If background music helps you focus, you may want to turn it on, but otherwise keep the room quiet. If you are using a computer to take notes, be sure you don't have any other windows open, especially applications like social media, games, or anything else that could distract you. Silence your phone and turn off notifications. Be sure to keep water close by so you stay hydrated while you study (but avoid unhealthy drinks and snacks).

Also, take into account the best time of day to study. Are you freshest first thing in the morning? Try to set aside some time then to work through the material. Is your mind clearer in the afternoon or evening? Schedule your study session then. Another method is to study at the same time of day that you will take the test, so that your brain gets used to working on the material at that time and will be ready to focus at test time.

STEP 5: STUDY!

Once you have done all the study preparation, it's time to settle into the actual studying. Sit down, take a few moments to settle your mind so you can focus, and begin to follow your study plan. Don't give in to distractions or let yourself procrastinate. This is your time to prepare so you'll be ready to fearlessly approach the test. Make the most of the time and stay focused.

Of course, you don't want to burn out. If you study too long you may find that you're not retaining the information very well. Take regular study breaks. For example, taking five minutes out of every hour to walk briskly, breathing deeply and swinging your arms, can help your mind stay fresh.

As you get to the end of each chapter or section, it's a good idea to do a quick review. Remind yourself of what you learned and work on any difficult parts. When you feel that you've mastered the material, move on to the next part. At the end of your study session, briefly skim through your notes again.

But while review is helpful, cramming last minute is NOT. If at all possible, work ahead so that you won't need to fit all your study into the last day. Cramming overloads your brain with more information than it can process and retain, and your tired mind may struggle to recall even previously learned information when it is overwhelmed with last-minute study. Also, the urgent nature of cramming and the stress placed on your brain contribute to anxiety. You'll be more likely to go to the test feeling unprepared and having trouble thinking clearly.

So don't cram, and don't stay up late before the test, even just to review your notes at a leisurely pace. Your brain needs rest more than it needs to go over the information again. In fact, plan to finish your studies by noon or early afternoon the day before the test. Give your brain the rest of the day to relax or focus on other things, and get a good night's sleep. Then you will be fresh for the test and better able to recall what you've studied.

STEP 6: TAKE A PRACTICE TEST

Many courses offer sample tests, either online or in the study materials. This is an excellent resource to check whether you have mastered the material, as well as to prepare for the test format and environment.

Check the test format ahead of time: the number of questions, the type (multiple choice, free response, etc.), and the time limit. Then create a plan for working through them. For example, if you have 30 minutes to take a 60-question test, your limit is 30 seconds per question. Spend less time on the questions you know well so that you can take more time on the difficult ones.

If you have time to take several practice tests, take the first one open book, with no time limit. Work through the questions at your own pace and make sure you fully understand them. Gradually work up to taking a test under test conditions: sit at a desk with all study materials put away and set a timer. Pace yourself to make sure you finish the test with time to spare and go back to check your answers if you have time.

After each test, check your answers. On the questions you missed, be sure you understand why you missed them. Did you misread the question (tests can use tricky wording)? Did you forget the information? Or was it something you hadn't learned? Go back and study any shaky areas that the practice tests reveal.

Taking these tests not only helps with your grade, but also aids in combating test anxiety. If you're already used to the test conditions, you're less likely to worry about it, and working through tests until you're scoring well gives you a confidence boost. Go through the practice tests until you feel comfortable, and then you can go into the test knowing that you're ready for it.

Test Tips

On test day, you should be confident, knowing that you've prepared well and are ready to answer the questions. But aside from preparation, there are several test day strategies you can employ to maximize your performance.

First, as stated before, get a good night's sleep the night before the test (and for several nights before that, if possible). Go into the test with a fresh, alert mind rather than staying up late to study.

Try not to change too much about your normal routine on the day of the test. It's important to eat a nutritious breakfast, but if you normally don't eat breakfast at all, consider eating just a protein bar. If you're a coffee drinker, go ahead and have your normal coffee. Just make sure you time it so that the caffeine doesn't wear off right in the middle of your test. Avoid sugary beverages, and drink enough water to stay hydrated but not so much that you need a restroom break 10 minutes into the test. If your test isn't first thing in the morning, consider going for a walk or doing a light workout before the test to get your blood flowing.

Allow yourself enough time to get ready, and leave for the test with plenty of time to spare so you won't have the anxiety of scrambling to arrive in time. Another reason to be early is to select a good seat. It's helpful to sit away from doors and windows, which can be distracting. Find a good seat, get out your supplies, and settle your mind before the test begins.

When the test begins, start by going over the instructions carefully, even if you already know what to expect. Make sure you avoid any careless mistakes by following the directions.

Then begin working through the questions, pacing yourself as you've practiced. If you're not sure on an answer, don't spend too much time on it, and don't let it shake your confidence. Either skip it and come back later, or eliminate as many wrong answers as possible and guess among the remaining ones. Don't dwell on these questions as you continue—put them out of your mind and focus on what lies ahead.

Be sure to read all of the answer choices, even if you're sure the first one is the right answer. Sometimes you'll find a better one if you keep reading. But don't second-guess yourself if you do immediately know the answer. Your gut instinct is usually right. Don't let test anxiety rob you of the information you know.

If you have time at the end of the test (and if the test format allows), go back and review your answers. Be cautious about changing any, since your first instinct tends to be correct, but make sure you didn't misread any of the questions or accidentally mark the wrong answer choice. Look over any you skipped and make an educated guess.

At the end, leave the test feeling confident. You've done your best, so don't waste time worrying about your performance or wishing you could change anything. Instead, celebrate the successful

completion of this test. And finally, use this test to learn how to deal with anxiety even better next time.

Important Qualification

Not all anxiety is created equal. If your test anxiety is causing major issues in your life beyond the classroom or testing center, or if you are experiencing troubling physical symptoms related to your anxiety, it may be a sign of a serious physiological or psychological condition. If this sounds like your situation, we strongly encourage you to seek professional help.

Tell Us Your Story

We at Mometrix would like to extend our heartfelt thanks to you for letting us be a part of your journey. It is an honor to serve people from all walks of life, people like you, who are committed to building the best future they can for themselves.

We know that each person's situation is unique. But we also know that, whether you are a young student or a mother of four, you care about working to make your own life and the lives of those around you better.

That's why we want to hear your story.

We want to know why you're taking this test. We want to know about the trials you've gone through to get here. And we want to know about the successes you've experienced after taking and passing your test.

In addition to your story, which can be an inspiration both to us and to others, we value your feedback. We want to know both what you loved about our book and what you think we can improve on.

The team at Mometrix would be absolutely thrilled to hear from you! So please, send us an email at tellusyourstory@mometrix.com or visit us at mometrix.com/tellusyourstory.php and let's stay in touch.

Additional Bonus Material

Due to our efforts to try to keep this book to a manageable length, we've created a link that will give you access to all of your additional bonus material:

mometrix.com/bonus948/lifehealth

CPSIA information can be obtained
at www.ICGtesting.com
Printed in the USA
LVHW011910260423
745400LV00003B/15